Schweser Weekly Class Workbook

2017 Level I CFA®

Volume 2

KAPLAN

SCHWESER

SCHWESER WEEKLY CLASS WORKBOOK: 2017 LEVEL I CFA®, VOLUME 2
©2016 Kaplan, Inc. All rights reserved.

Published in September 2016 by Kaplan Schweser.
Printed in the United States of America.

ISBN: 978-1-4754-4206-9

Contents

Study Session 10

Corporate Finance: Corporate Governance, Capital Budgeting, and Cost of Capital

Corporate Governance, Capital Budgeting, and Cost of Capital

34. Corporate Governance and ESG: An Introduction

KAPLAN UNIVERSITY SCHOOL OF PROFESSIONAL AND CONTINUING EDUCATION | SCHWESER

Study Session 10
Corporate Governance, Capital Budgeting, and Cost of Capital

34. Corporate Governance and ESG: An Introduction
35. Capital Budgeting
36. Cost of Capital

KAPLAN UNIVERSITY SCHOOL OF PROFESSIONAL AND CONTINUING EDUCATION | SCHWESER

LOS 34.b Describe/Compare
CFAI p. 8, Schweser p. 2

Stakeholder Groups

LOS 34.a Describe
CFAI p. 6, Schweser p. 1

Corporate Governance

Corporate governance: Internal controls and procedures for managing a company

Shareholder theory: Focus on interests of company's owners

Stakeholder theory: Focus on managing conflicts among interests of *stakeholder groups*

Principal-Agent Relationships

An **agent** is hired to act in the interests of a **principal**

Shareholders (principals) use agents to run a company (i.e., elect directors who appoint senior managers)

Conflicts may arise between agents' interests and principals' interests

Example: Directors and managers may choose lower risk level than shareholders want

© Kaplan, Inc.

4

Stakeholder Management

Legal infrastructure: Laws relevant to stakeholders

Contractual infrastructure: Contracts between company and stakeholders

Organizational infrastructure: Corporate governance processes, management of stakeholder relationships

Governmental infrastructure: Regulations under which company operates

© Kaplan, Inc.

5

Stakeholder Management

Relationship with *shareholders*:

- Annual general meeting
- Extraordinary general meetings—special resolutions
- Proxy voting

Majority: One vote per share for each board seat

Cumulative: Votes = shares × seats, may cast all votes for one board candidate

© Kaplan, Inc.

6

Board of Directors

One-tier board:

Includes internal directors (senior managers) and external directors (*independent directors* if they have no other relationship with company)

Two-tier board:

Supervisory board (external directors) and *management board* (internal directors)

© Kaplan, Inc.

7

Slide 8

Board of Directors

Board responsibilities:

- Set strategic direction for company
- Select and evaluate senior managers, set their compensation, and plan for succession
- Approve large investments, acquisitions, and changes in capital structure
- Establish and monitor internal controls
- Ensure quality of financial reporting through internal and external auditors

© Kaplan, Inc.

8

Slide 9

Board Committees

Audit: Oversee financial reporting, internal controls, and internal audit; recommend external auditor to Board

Governance: Implement company code of ethics; monitor changes in laws and regulations and ensure company's compliance

Nominations: Search for and propose candidates for Board; align Board compensation with company goals

© Kaplan, Inc.

9

Slide 10

Board Committees

Compensation (Remuneration): Recommend compensation levels and types for directors and senior managers; oversee employee benefit plans

Risk: Recommend appropriate risk policy and risk tolerance; oversee risk management processes

Investment: Review proposed capital investment projects, acquisitions, and asset sales

© Kaplan, Inc.

10

Slide 11

Factors Affecting Stakeholder Relationships

Market factors:

Pressure from **activist shareholders** for changes they believe will increase company value

Threat of **hostile takeover**

© Kaplan, Inc.

11

Factors Affecting Stakeholder Relationships

Non-market factors:

Legal environment—Civil or common-law systems

Communications channels—Social media has increased dissident shareholders' ability to influence public opinion

Third-party ratings of corporate governance

Risks of Poor Corporate Governance

May decrease company value through:

- Weak controls (audits, board oversight)
- Poor or fraudulent accounting
- Lax oversight of management: Sub-optimal risk levels, related-party transactions, or compensation not aligned with company goals
  - Legal and reputational risks

Analysis of Corporate Governance

Ownership: Holdings by affiliated companies or institutions, activist shareholders, or company founders (*dual-class structure* may favor interests of one group of shareholders over others)

Board composition: Director independence from management; expertise suited to company's strategy

Analysis of Corporate Governance

Management compensation: Alignment with company strategy; long-term or short-term focus; stability over time (performance targets too easy?)

Shareholder rights: Weaker with staggered boards, anti-takeover provisions, or dual share classes

Environmental and Social Considerations

ESG integration: Considering environmental, social, and governance factors when making investment decisions

Also called *sustainable investing* or *responsible investing*

© Kaplan, Inc.

16

ESG in Investment Analysis

Negative screening: Excluding companies or sectors based on ESG factors

Positive screening: Identify companies with best practices related to ESG factors

Impact investing: Seek to profit while having positive impact on a social or environmental goal

Thematic investing: Based on a specific ESG factor

© Kaplan, Inc.

17

Corporate Governance, Capital Budgeting, and Cost of Capital

35. Capital Budgeting

KAPLAN UNIVERSITY SCHOOL OF PROFESSIONAL AND CONTINUING EDUCATION | SCHWESER

Capital Budgeting Process

The **capital budgeting process** is used to determine and select (the most) profitable long-term (greater than one year) projects.

© Kaplan, Inc.

19

Steps in the Capital Budgeting Process

Step 1: Idea generation

Step 2: Analyze project proposals

Step 3: Create capital budget for the firm

Step 4: Monitor decisions, conduct a post-audit

© Kaplan, Inc.

20

Types of Capital Projects

■ Replacement projects to maintain the business

■ Replacement projects for cost reduction

■ Capacity expansion projects

■ New products or markets

■ Mandatory projects—safety and environment

   ■ Other projects: Pet projects, R&D

© Kaplan, Inc.

21

Principles of Capital Budgeting

■ Decisions are made based on the changes in after-tax cash flows

■ Do not consider **sunk costs** or any project-specific financing costs—financing costs are in discount rate used

■ Consider cash **opportunity costs**

■ Consider **externalities**—cannibalization

   ■ **Timing** of cash flows is important

© Kaplan, Inc.

22

Project Interactions

■ Independent projects vs. mutually exclusive projects

■ Project sequencing—opportunity for profitable future projects

   ■ Unlimited funds vs. capital rationing

© Kaplan, Inc.

23

Net Present Value (NPV)

For simple project: PV of cash flows – initial cost

$$NPV = CF_0 + \frac{CF_1}{(1+k)^1} + \frac{CF_2}{(1+k)^2} + \cdots + \frac{CF_n}{(1+k)^n}$$

End of Year	Cash Flows	Discounted @9%
0	–$100	–$100.00
1	25	22.94
2	50	42.08
3	75	57.91
		NPV = $22.93

© Kaplan, Inc.

24

Net Present Value (NPV)

- NPV indicates the expected change in the value of the firm, in current (PV) dollars

- Accepting projects with NPV > 0 is expected to increase shareholder wealth

- Accepting a zero NPV project will not increase shareholder wealth

Decision rule for <u>independent projects</u>:
Accept all projects with NPV > 0

© Kaplan, Inc.

25

Internal Rate of Return (IRR)

IRR is the expected return on the project

IRR is the discount rate for which the PV of the project's CFs is equal to the initial outlay (makes the NPV = 0)

$$NPV = 0 = CF_0 + \frac{CF_1}{(1+IRR)^1} + \frac{CF_2}{(1+IRR)^2} + \cdots + \frac{CF_n}{(1+IRR)^n}$$

© Kaplan, Inc.

26

Internal Rate of Return (IRR)

Use the CF keys on your calculator.

End of Year	Cash Flows	Discounted @ 19.4%
0	–$100	–$100.00
1	25	20.94
2	50	35.07
3	75	44.06
		$\Sigma = 0.00 = NPV$

Because NPV = 0
IRR = 19.4%

© Kaplan, Inc.

27

Internal Rate of Return (IRR)

Decision rule for <u>independent projects</u>:

Accept all projects with an IRR > cost of capital (hurdle rate)

<u>This rule is equivalent to NPV > 0</u>

If NPV > 0 or IRR > cost of capital, then PV of cash flows > initial outlay.

© Kaplan, Inc.   28

Payback Period

Primarily a measure of liquidity

Projects with payback periods longer than a given number of years are rejected

Limitations

- Not a measure of value
- Ignores time value of money
- Ignores CFs beyond the payback period

© Kaplan, Inc.   29

Payback Period

Example:

End of Year	Cash Flows	Cumulative Cash Flows
0	–$100	–$100
1	25	–75
2	50	–25
3	75	50

Payback period = 2 + 25 / 75 = 2.333 years

Firm recovers its initial investment in 2.333 years.

© Kaplan, Inc.   30

Discounted Payback Period (DPP)

End of Year	Cash Flows	Discounted @9%	Cumulative Discounted Cash Flows
0	–$100	–$100.00	–$100.00
1	25	22.94	–77.06
2	50	42.08	–34.98
3	75	57.91	22.93

DPP = 2 + 34.98 / 57.91 = 2.6 years

Ignores CFs after payback

Both payback methods focus on liquidity

© Kaplan, Inc.   31

Profitability Index (PI)

Present value of future cash flows divided by initial cash outlay

$$PI = \frac{PV \; Future \; CF}{CF_0} = 1 + \frac{NPV}{CF_0}$$

Decision rule for independent projects:
   Accept all projects for which PI > 1

If NPV > 0, then IRR > discount rate and PI > 1

© Kaplan, Inc.   32

NPV Profile

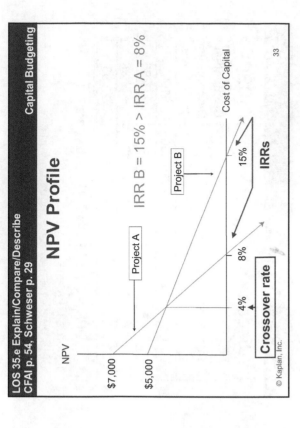

Project A   IRR B = 15% > IRR A = 8%

IRR B = 15%

Crossover rate

© Kaplan, Inc.   33

IRR vs. NPV Project Rankings

For **independent projects**, IRR and NPV rules give the **same** accept/reject decisions

For **mutually exclusive projects**, IRR and NPV project rankings may differ, when:

   • Projects have different timing of CFs
   • The projects (CF_0) are different sizes

Difference in reinvestment rate assumptions:

   ▪ IRR assumes CFs reinvested at project's IRR
   ▪ NPV assumes CFs reinvested at the cost of capital (more conservative)

© Kaplan, Inc.   34

The Multiple/No IRR Problem

Potential problems if project's cash flows change signs more than once:

Multiple IRRs – More than one IRR will make NPV = 0

No IRR – There is no IRR that will make NPV = 0

NPV method does not have these problems

© Kaplan, Inc.   35

Corporate Governance, Capital Budgeting, and Cost of Capital

36. Cost of Capital

KAPLAN
UNIVERSITY   SCHOOL OF PROFESSIONAL
AND CONTINUING EDUCATION | SCHWESER

LOS 35.f Describe
CFAI p. 63, Schweser p. 32

Relationship Between NPV and Stock Price

NPV is a direct measure of the expected change in shareholder wealth from a project

Estimate increase in share value as NPV divided by number of shares

In practice, only unexpected opportunities will increase expected future cash flows and value

© Kaplan, Inc.

36

LOS 36.a.b Calculate/Interpret/Describe
CFAI p. 74, Schweser p. 41

Weighted-Average Cost of Capital

k_d Yield-to-maturity on existing/new debt; before-tax cost of debt

$k_d(1 - t)$ After-tax cost of debt, where t is the marginal tax rate—only interest on debt is paid pre-tax

k_{ps} Cost of preferred stock

k_{ce} Cost of common equity

© Kaplan, Inc.

39

LOS 36.a Calculate/Interpret
CFAI p. 74, Schweser p. 41

Weighted-Average Cost of Capital

The overall opportunity cost of the firm's capital is a weighted average of the opportunity costs of capital from **debt, preferred equity, and common equity**

Project should be undertaken only if the return on invested capital is **greater than its opportunity cost of capital**

© Kaplan, Inc.

38

Weighted-Average Cost of Capital (WACC)

$WACC = (w_d)[k_d(1 - t)] + (w_{ps})(k_{ps}) + (w_{ce})(k_{ce})$

Example: Firm X target capital structure is 10% preferred, 45% debt, and 45% common equity

$k_d = 7.5\%$, $t = 40\%$, $k_{ps} = 9.0\%$, and $k_{ce} = 11.5\%$

$WACC = 0.45 \times 7.5\% (1 - 0.4) + 0.1 \times 9.0\% + 0.45 \times 11.5\% = 8.1\%$

© Kaplan, Inc.   40

Target (Optimal) Capital Structure

Target capital structure: The proportions (based on market values) of debt, preferred stock, and equity that the firm expects to achieve over time

How do analysts determine target weights?

- Can use existing capital structure weights
- Can adjust existing weights for firm trends
- Can use industry average weights

© Kaplan, Inc.   41

Marginal Cost of Capital (MCC)

- A firm's MCC is the cost of an additional dollar of capital

- MCC is the WACC of the next dollar of capital raised

- A firm's MCC increases as the firm increases the amount of capital it raises during a given period

- Thus, the **marginal cost of capital curve** slopes upward

© Kaplan, Inc.   42

Optimal Capital Budget

- Given the expected returns (IRRs) on potential projects, we can order the **opportunities for investment** highest to lowest IRR

- This will allow us to construct a downward-sloping **investment opportunity schedule**

- The intersection of the investment opportunity schedule with the marginal cost of capital curve identifies the **optimal capital budget**

© Kaplan, Inc.   43

Role of the WACC/MCC in Determining NPV of Projects

The WACC is the appropriate discount rate (cost of capital) for projects that have the same level of risk as the firm's existing projects

- For a project with above-average risk, discount rate > WACC

- For projects with below-average risk, discount rate < WACC

© Kaplan, Inc.   45

The Cost of Debt

- When available, use the **market rate of interest (YTM)** on firm's current debt for k_d

- If firm debt is not publicly traded, estimate the YTM using the **debt rating and maturity of existing debt**

- For firms that primarily use floating-rate debt, estimate the longer-term cost of the firm's debt using the **current yield curve** and firm's debt rating

© Kaplan, Inc.   47

Optimal Capital Budget

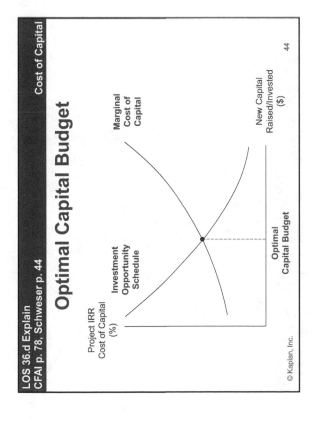

© Kaplan, Inc.   44

The Cost of Debt

k_d = current market YTM = pre-tax cost of debt
After-tax cost of debt = k_d (1 – marginal tax rate)

Example: Firm X can issue new par debt at an interest rate of 7.5%. If the firm has a 40% marginal tax rate, what is Firm X's after-tax cost of debt?

After-tax cost of debt = 7.5% (1 – 0.4) = 4.5%

© Kaplan, Inc.   46

Cost of Capital

The Cost of Preferred Stock

$$k_{ps} = \frac{\text{preferred dividend}}{\text{market price of preferred}}$$

Example: New noncallable, nonconvertible preferred stock with a dividend of $8.50 has a value of $100/share. What is the firm's cost of preferred stock?

$$k_{ps} = \$8.50 \, / \, \$100.00 = 0.085 = 8.5\%$$

© Kaplan, Inc.

48

Cost of Capital

The Cost of Common Equity

Method 1: CAPM

$$\text{CAPM: } k_{ce} = Rf + \beta[E(R_{mkt}) - Rf]$$

where: Rf = risk-free rate (match to project length)

β = beta (systematic risk) of firm's stock

$E(R_{mkt})$ = expected market return

Example: Rf = 5%, the expected return on the market is 11%, and Firm X's beta is 1.1

$$k_{ce} = 5\% + 1.1 \, (11\% - 5\%) = 11.6\%$$

© Kaplan, Inc.

49

Cost of Capital

The Cost of Common Equity

Method 2: Dividend Discount Approach

$$k_{ce} = \frac{D_1}{P_0} + g$$

D_1 = **next year's** dividend

P_0 = current stock price

g = firm's expected constant growth rate

= (ROE)(retention rate)

© Kaplan, Inc.

50

Cost of Capital

The Cost of Common Equity

Method 3: Bond yield plus risk premium

$$k_{ce} = \text{bond market yield} + \text{risk premium}$$

(e.g., k_{ce} = 7.5% + 4% = 11.5%)

- Assumes investors require a higher return on a firm's equity than on its debt
- Risk premium normally ranges from 3% to 5%
- Based on judgment, imprecise

© Kaplan, Inc.

51

LOS 36.i Calculate/Interpret
CFAI p. 90, Schweser p. 49

Cost of Capital for a Project

Which of the following methods for estimating the weights for calculating a firm's WACC is *least* acceptable?

A. Current proportions of debt and equity based on balance sheet values.

B. Industry average weights for debt and equity.

C. Firm's announced target capital structure weights.

© Kaplan, Inc.

52 - 1

LOS 36.i Calculate/Interpret
CFAI p. 90, Schweser p. 49

Cost of Capital for a Project

- Calculate cost of equity for the project using the pure play method

- Calculate the cost of debt for the company

- Calculate the cost of capital for the project using the debt/equity ratio of the subject company and the WACC formula

© Kaplan, Inc.

53

LOS 36.i Calculate/Interpret
CFAI p. 90, Schweser p. 49

Cost of Capital for a Project

Pure play method steps:

1. Calculate the beta of a comparable company (or companies) that is a pure play in the industry

2. Unlever it to adjust for differences in debt/equity ratio—this is the asset beta

3. Relever it to reflect the debt/equity ratio of the subject company—this is the project beta

4. Use the project beta as the cost of equity for the project when calculating WACC

© Kaplan, Inc.

54

LOS 36.i Calculate/Interpret
CFAI p. 90, Schweser p. 49

Asset Beta

Asset (unlevered) beta:

$$\beta_{ASSET} = \beta_{PURE\ PLAY} \left[\frac{1}{1 + \left((1-t)\dfrac{D}{E} \right)} \right]$$

where: D/E is the *pure play company's* debt-to-equity ratio and *t* is its marginal tax rate

© Kaplan, Inc.

55

Calculate the Company (Project) Beta

Company (project) beta:

$$\beta_{PROJECT} = \beta_{ASSET}\left[1+\left((1-t)\frac{D}{E}\right)\right]$$

Use the *subject firm's* tax rate and debt-to-equity ratio to re-lever the asset beta

© Kaplan, Inc.   56

Pure Play Method Example

Carl Industries is considering an investment in robotics, which is outside their current business activities. To estimate the cost of equity for this project, they have identified a public company that is exclusively involved in robotics design and manufacturing, Robotic Solutions (RS). The relevant information is:

	Carl	RS
Beta	1.2	1.5
Equity/Assets	55%	40%
Tax rate	35%	20%

Rf is 3%, and the equity risk premium is 5%.

What cost of equity should Carl use for the robotics project?

© Kaplan, Inc.   57

Pure Play Method Example

$$\beta_{ASSET} = 1.5\left[\frac{1}{1+\left((1-0.2)\frac{0.6}{0.4}\right)}\right] = 0.68$$

$$\beta_{PROJECT} = 0.68\left[1+\left((1-0.35)\frac{0.45}{0.55}\right)\right] = 1.04$$

Cost of equity for project = 3% + 1.04(5%) = 8.2%

© Kaplan, Inc.   58

Country Risk Premium

Problem: CAPM is problematic for estimating project cost of equity in developing markets

Solution: Add country risk premium (CRP) to market risk premium when using CAPM

$$k_{ce} = R_F + \beta\left[E(R_{MKT}) - R_F + CRP\right]$$

© Kaplan, Inc.   59

Marginal Cost of Capital (MCC)

MCC: Opportunity cost of using an additional dollar of capital; WACC of raising an additional dollar

- Cost of each source of capital will increase at some level of new capital raised, these are breakpoints

  - The result is an **upward-sloping MCC schedule**

© Kaplan, Inc.   60

MCC and Investment Opportunity Schedules

© Kaplan, Inc.   61

Calculating Breakpoints

The amount of new capital investment for which the WACC increases because the cost of one of the component costs of capital increases is termed a "breakpoint" and is:

$$\frac{\text{Amount of capital at which the component's cost of capital changes}}{\text{Weight of the component in the the capital structure}}$$

(e.g., cost of debt increases at $1.5 million raised, debt is 30% : breakpoint = 1.5 / 0.3 = $5 million)

© Kaplan, Inc.   62

Flotation Costs

Flotation costs are fees charged by investment bankers when a company sells equity shares

Range from 2% to 7% of the capital raised

Wrong way: Adjust cost of equity

Cost is incorrectly spread over life of project

Right way: Adjust initial outflow for flotation costs

Treats flotation cost as a single cash outflow at project inception

© Kaplan, Inc.   63

Additional Problems

Additional Problems

2) Cash flows for two projects are as follows:

t=0	t=1	t=2	t=3	t=4	t=5	t=6
–100	25	25	25	25	25	75
–100	50	25	25	25	25	25

The discount rate at which their present values will be equal is *closest* to:

A. 13%.

B. 15%.

C. 17%.

- 5

Cost of Capital

At the beginning of last year, Acme Inc. had equity of $2 million and a share price of $15. For the year, net income was $200,000, dividends were $0.30/sh. on 200,000 outstanding shares. Acme's cost of equity capital is:

64 - 3

Additional Problems

1) A project has an initial outlay of $2.1 million and cash flows each year for 8 years of $350,000. If the required rate of return is 5%, the PI for this project is *closest* to:

A. 1.08.

B. 1.11.

C. 1.18.

- 3

Additional Problems

3) The threat of a hostile takeover is *most likely* to:

A. lead to an improvement in corporate governance.

B. motivate senior managers to maximize firm value.

C. come from dissatisfied management.

- 2

© Kaplan, Inc.

STUDY SESSION 10 ANSWERS

Reading	Slide Number	Answer
36	52	A
36	64	9%

Additional Problems

1. A

2. B

3. B

Study Session 11

Corporate Finance: Leverage, Dividends and Share Repurchases, and Working Capital Management

---

Corporate Finance

Study Session 11

Leverage, Dividends and Share Repurchases, and Working Capital Management

37. Measures of Leverage
38. Dividends and Share Repurchases: Basics
39. Working Capital Management

KAPLAN UNIVERSITY | SCHOOL OF PROFESSIONAL AND CONTINUING EDUCATION | SCHWESER

© Kaplan, Inc.

Corporate Finance

Leverage, Dividends and Share Repurchases, and Working Capital Management

37. Measures of Leverage

KAPLAN UNIVERSITY | SCHOOL OF PROFESSIONAL AND CONTINUING EDUCATION | SCHWESER

Measures of Leverage

LOS 37.a Define/Explain/Classify
CFAI p. 122, Schweser p. 66

Definitions

Leverage: Refers to the effect of fixed elements in cost structure

   Operating leverage: Fixed operating expenses

   Financial leverage: Fixed financing costs

Business risk: Variability in EBIT from operating leverage (and variability of revenue and expenses)

Financial risk: Additional variability of EPS from fixed interest costs

© Kaplan, Inc.

2

Measures of Leverage

LOS 37.b Calculate/Interpret
CFAI p. 124, Schweser p. 67

Degree of Operating Leverage (DOL)

Definition/Interpretation:

$$DOL = \frac{\% \text{ change in EBIT}}{\% \text{ change in sales}}$$

Calculation:

$$DOL = \frac{sales - TVC}{sales - TVC - fixed}$$

When fixed costs are zero, DOL = 1, there is no operating leverage so $\% \Delta$ EBIT = $\% \Delta$ sales

© Kaplan, Inc.

3

Degree of Operating Leverage (DOL)

A firm's fixed costs are $70,000, its selling price was $75/unit, and its variable cost is $50/unit. What is the firm's DOL at 5,000 units of output?

$$DOL = \frac{Sales - TVC}{Sales - TVC - Fixed} = \frac{Q(P - V_{Unit})}{Q(P - V_{Unit}) - Fixed}$$

$$= \frac{5,000(75 - 50)}{5,000(75 - 50) - 70,000} = 2.27$$

© Kaplan, Inc.   4 - 1

Degree of Financial Leverage (DFL)

Definition/Interpretation: $DFL = \dfrac{\% \text{ change in EPS}}{\% \text{ change in EBIT}}$

Calculation: $DFL = \dfrac{EBIT}{EBIT - interest}$

When fixed financing costs are zero, DFL = 1, there is no financial leverage so %Δ EPS = %Δ EBIT

© Kaplan, Inc.   5

Degree of Financial Leverage (DFL)

A firm has EBIT of $55,000 and interest expense of $20,000. If EBIT increases by 3%, what will be the effect on earnings per share?

$$DFL = \frac{55,000}{55,000 - 20,000} = 1.57$$

EPS will increase by 3% × 1.57 = **4.71%**

© Kaplan, Inc.   6 - 2

Degree of Total Leverage (DTL)

Definition/Interpretation: $DTL = \dfrac{\% \text{ change in EPS}}{\% \text{ change in sales}}$

$$DTL = DOL \times DFL$$

Two sources of leverage; multiplicative

$$DTL = \frac{Q(P - V)}{Q(P - V) - fixed - interest}$$

$$= \frac{sales - TVC}{sales - TVC - fixed - interest}$$

© Kaplan, Inc.   7

Degree of Total Leverage (DTL)

What is the DTL of a firm that had sales last year of $375,000, total variable costs of $250,000, fixed costs of $70,000, and interest expense of $20,000?

$$DTL = \frac{sales - TVC}{sales - TVC - fixed - interest}$$

$$= \frac{375,000 - 250,000}{375,000 - 250,000 - 70,000 - 20,000} = 3.57$$

$$DOL \times DFL = DTL; \quad 2.27 \times 1.57 = 3.57$$

© Kaplan, Inc.   8 – 1

Firm Characteristics and Leverage

Three rules of leverage:

1. High fixed costs = high operating leverage

2. High debt ratio = high financial leverage

3. High fixed costs + high debt ratio = high total leverage

© Kaplan, Inc.   9

Polsen, Inc. has fixed operating costs of $1.5 million, fixed financing costs of $1.0 million, sells their output at $700 per unit, and has variable costs of $200 per unit. At an output of 5,000 units, a decrease in sales of 1% can be expected to decrease operating earnings by:

A. 1.0%.

B. 2.5%.

C. 3.5%.

© Kaplan, Inc.   10 – 2

Breakeven Quantity of Sales

Breakeven quantity is the level of sales at which a firm's net income is zero

$$Q_{BE} = \frac{Total\ Fixed\ Costs}{Price - Var.\ Cost\ per\ unit}$$

If P = $85; V = $60; FC = $500,000;
What is the firm's breakeven quantity of sales?

$$\boxed{Q_{BE} = 500,000 / (85 - 60) = 20,000\ units}$$

© Kaplan, Inc.   11 – 1

LOS 37.d Calculate/Determine
CFAI p. 139, Schweser p. 72   Measures of Leverage

Net Income at Various Sales Levels

For a firm, P = $85; VC = $60; FOC = $500,000;
Interest = $20,000; Q = 25,000 units, no taxes

What is the firm's pre-tax income?

Income = Q(P – V) – fixed costs – interest

25,000(85 – 60) – 500,000 – 20,000 = $105,000

© Kaplan, Inc.   12 - 2

LOS 37.e Calculate/Interpret
CFAI p. 139, Schweser p. 72   Measures of Leverage

Operating Breakeven Quantity of Sales

__Operating breakeven quantity__ is the level of sales
that just covers a firm's fixed operating costs

$$Q_{OBE} = \frac{Fixed\ Operating\ Costs}{Price - Var.\ Cost\ per\ unit}$$

If P = $85, V = $60, fixed operating costs =
$300,000, what is the firm's operating breakeven
quantity of sales?

$Q_{OBE} = 300,000 / (85 - 60) = 12,000\ units$

© Kaplan, Inc.   13 - 1

Corporate Finance

Leverage, Dividends and Share Repurchases, and Working Capital Management

38.Dividends and Share Repurchases: Basics

LOS 38.a Describe
CFAI p. 152, Schweser p. 81   Dividends and Share
                                      Repurchases: Basics

Types of Dividends

Cash dividends: Payments made to
shareholders in cash

Three types:

- Regular dividends
- Special dividends
- Liquidating dividends

© Kaplan, Inc.   15

LOS 38.a Describe
CFAI p. 152, Schweser p. 81

Dividends and Share
Repurchases: Basics

Stock Dividends, Stock Splits

Stock dividend: Payment to shareholders in shares of stock (e.g., 10% of existing shares)

Stock split: Proportionate *increase* in shares outstanding (e.g., 2 for 1)

Reverse stock split: Proportionate *decrease* in shares outstanding (e.g., 1 for 5)

Stock splits and stock dividends do not change value of stock outstanding

© Kaplan, Inc.   16

LOS 38.a Describe
CFAI p. 152, Schweser p. 81

Dividends and Share
Repurchases: Basics

Effects on Financial Ratios

Cash dividend:
Assets ↓ (cash)
Equity ↓ (retained earnings)

Liquidity ratios decrease due to decrease in cash (current assets)

Leverage ratios increase due to decreases in assets, equity

Stock dividends, stock splits do not affect liquidity ratios or leverage ratios

© Kaplan, Inc.   17

LOS 38.b Describe
CFAI p. 160, Schweser p. 84

Dividends and Share
Repurchases: Basics

Dividend Payment Procedures

Date board announces dividend

First day stock trades without dividend, price down by ≈ dividend

Holder of record date   Payment date

Declaration date   Ex-dividend date

August 25   September 15   September 17   September 30

Date shareholders must own to receive dividend

Date checks are mailed or funds electronically transferred

© Kaplan, Inc.   18

LOS 38.c Compare
CFAI p. 163, Schweser p. 85

Dividends and Share
Repurchases: Basics

Share Repurchase Methods

Open market repurchase
- Buy at market price in the open market
- Flexibility in timing

Tender offer
- Buy fixed number of shares at fixed price
- Typically at a premium to market
- May use Dutch auction to determine price

Direct negotiation
Typically at a premium to market

© Kaplan, Inc.   19

Share Repurchase

Rationales for share repurchase instead of cash dividend:

1. Tax advantage to shareholders if tax rate on capital gains < tax rate on dividends

2. Signal to shareholders that management believes shares are undervalued

© Kaplan, Inc.

20

Share Repurchase With Borrowed Funds

Price = $50/share, 50,000 shares outstanding

EPS = $4, after-tax cost of funds = 10%

Buy back 5,000 shares | Earnings yield = 4 / 50 = 8% |

Interest cost = 5,000 × $50 × 10% = $25,000

$$\text{new EPS} = \frac{\$4(50,000) - \$25,000}{50,000 - 5,000} = \$3.89 / sh.$$

| When after-tax cost of funds is **greater** than earnings yield (EPS/Price), EPS falls |

© Kaplan, Inc.

21

Share Repurchase Effect on BVPS

Price = $50/share, 50,000 shares outstanding

BVPS = $40, buy back 5,000 shares

Buyback amount = 5,000 × 50 = $250,000

Original equity = 50,000 × 40 = $2,000,000

$$\text{new BVPS} = \frac{\$2,000,000 - \$250,000}{50,000 - 5,000} = \$38.89 / sh.$$

| When share price is **greater** than book value, a repurchase **decreases** BV per share |

© Kaplan, Inc.

22

Share Repurchase vs. Cash Dividend

If tax treatment and information effects are the same, the effects of a cash dividend or a share repurchase in an equal amount are **the same**

Stock price = $30   10,000 shares outstanding

Pay a cash dividend of $3 per share = $30,000

Stock price = $30 – $3 = $27

Market value of equity = 10,000 × 27 = **$270,000**

Repurchase 1,000 shares for $30,000

Shares outstanding decrease to 9,000

Market value of equity = 9,000 × 30 = **$270,000**

© Kaplan, Inc.

23 - 2

Corporate Finance

Leverage, Dividends and Share Repurchases, and Working Capital Management

39. Working Capital Management

KAPLAN
UNIVERSITY

SCHOOL OF PROFESSIONAL
AND CONTINUING EDUCATION | SCHWESER

**Working Capital
Management**

LOS 39.a Describe
CFAI p. 182, Schweser p. 95

Sources of Liquidity

Primary Sources (from normal operations):

- Cash, cash equivalents, collections, and investment income

- Trade credit, bank lines of credit, and short-term investment portfolios

Secondary Sources (may significantly change firm):

  Renegotiation of debt, liquidation of assets, bankruptcy

© Kaplan, Inc.

25

**Working Capital
Management**

LOS 39.a Describe
CFAI p. 182, Schweser p. 95

Factors Influencing Liquidity

- Effectiveness of cash management

- Centralization of collections

- Liquidity of short- and long-term assets

© Kaplan, Inc.

26

**Working Capital
Management**

LOS 39.b Compare
CFAI p. 185, Schweser p. 96

Ratios

$$\text{Current ratio} = \frac{\text{Current assets}}{\text{Current liabilities}}$$

$$\text{Quick ratio} = \frac{\text{Cash} + \text{ST securities} + \text{receivables}}{\text{Current liabilities}}$$

$$\text{Cash ratio} = \frac{\text{Cash} + \text{ST securities}}{\text{Current liabilities}}$$

© Kaplan, Inc.

27

Slide 28

Ratios

$$\text{Receivables turnover} = \frac{\text{Credit sales}}{\text{Average receivables}}$$

$$\text{Inventory turnover} = \frac{\text{Cost of goods sold}}{\text{Average inventory}}$$

$$\text{Payables turnover} = \frac{\text{Purchases}}{\text{Average trade payables}}$$

© Kaplan, Inc.   28

Slide 29

Ratios

$$\text{\# days of receivables} = \frac{365}{\text{Receivables turnover}}$$

$$\text{\# days of inventory} = \frac{365}{\text{Inventory turnover}}$$

$$\text{\# days of payables} = \frac{365}{\text{Payables turnover}}$$

© Kaplan, Inc.   29

Slide 30

Operating and Cash Conversion Cycles

Operating cycle   = days of inventory
                          + days of receivables

Cash conversion cycle = days of inventory
                              + days of receivables
                              − days of payables

Cash conversion cycle is also called
net operating cycle here

© Kaplan, Inc.   30

Slide 31

Operating and Cash Conversion Cycles

Buy
raw materials

Sell goods
on credit

Collect
cash

Inventory days

Receivables days

OPERATING CYCLE

Payables days

CASH CONVERSION CYCLE

© Kaplan, Inc.   31

LOS 39.d Describe
CFAI p. 190, Schweser p. 98

Working Capital Management

Managing Net Daily Cash

Goal: Keep enough cash for routine needs, but not so much cash that the firm foregoes interest income

Forecast cash inflows and outflows by type
(e.g., sales, collections, purchases, wages, taxes, interest, dividends, transfers to/from subsidiaries)

- Short-term horizon: Next few weeks
- Medium-term horizon: Next 12 months
- Long-term horizon: Multi-year

© Kaplan, Inc.

32

LOS 39.e Calculate/Interpret/Compare/Evaluate
CFAI p. 195, Schweser p. 99

Working Capital Management

Short-term Investments

Invest excess cash in **short-term securities**:

- U.S. Treasury bills
- Short-term federal agency securities
- Bank certificates of deposit
- Banker's acceptances
- Time deposits
- Repurchase agreements
- Commercial paper
- Money market mutual funds
- Adjustable-rate preferred stock

© Kaplan, Inc.

33

LOS 39.e Calculate/Interpret/Compare/Evaluate
CFAI p. 195, Schweser p. 99

Working Capital Management

Comparing Short-term Yields

$$\% \text{ discount} = \frac{\text{Face value} - \text{price}}{\text{Face value}}$$

Discount basis (bank discount) yield = % discount $\times \dfrac{360}{\text{Days}}$

$$\text{Money market yield} = \left(\frac{\text{Face value} - \text{price}}{\text{Price}}\right)\left(\frac{360}{\text{Days}}\right) = \text{HPY} \times \frac{360}{\text{Days}}$$

$$\text{Bond equivalent yield} = \left(\frac{\text{Face value} - \text{price}}{\text{Price}}\right)\left(\frac{365}{\text{Days}}\right) = \text{HPY} \times \frac{365}{\text{Days}}$$

© Kaplan, Inc.

34

LOS 39.e Calculate/Interpret/Compare/Evaluate
CFAI p. 195, Schweser p. 99

Working Capital Management

Cash Management IPS

- Purpose and objective of investment portfolio
- Strategy guidelines
- Types of securities
- Individuals responsible for the portfolio
- Corrective steps
- Limitations

© Kaplan, Inc.

35

Accounts Receivable Aging Schedule
$ 000's

Days Outstanding	Mar	Apr	May
< 31 days	200	212	195
31–60 days	150	165	140
61–90 days	100	90	92
> 90 days	50	70	66

Can also be presented as percentage of total receivables

© Kaplan, Inc.

36

Weighted-Average Collection Period

Days Outstanding	Average Collection Days	% Weight	Days × Weight
< 31 days	22	40%	8.8
31–60 days	44	30%	13.2
61–90 days	74	20%	14.8
> 90 days	135	10%	13.5
Weighted-average collection period			**50.3**

© Kaplan, Inc.

37

Evaluating Performance

Receivables: Trade-off between credit terms and sales

Inventories: Too little can lead to stock-outs, too much increases carrying costs

Payables: Early payment can take advantage of discounts but gives up potential interest on cash; late payment increases interest costs, can damage supplier relationships

© Kaplan, Inc.

38

Sources of Short-term Funding

Lines of credit

- Committed: Requires fee
- Revolving: Fee, larger, strongest (U.S.)
- Uncommitted: Less reliable, no fee (U.S.)

Commercial paper: Large, strong credit

Bankers' acceptances: Import/export

Factoring: Smaller users, higher fees

Nonbank finance companies: Weak credit

© Kaplan, Inc.

39

Corporate Finance

Additional Problems

KAPLAN UNIVERSITY
SCHOOL OF PROFESSIONAL AND CONTINUING EDUCATION | SCHWESER

-4

CFA Curriculum Vol. 4, R.39, Q.2, p. 222

2) Given the following financial statement data, calculate the operating cycle for this company.

Credit sales = 25,000
Cost of goods sold = 20,000
Accounts receivable = 2,500
Inventory—Beginning balance = 2,000
Inventory—Ending balance = 2,300
Accounts payable = 1,700
The operating cycle for this company is *closest* to:

A. 42.0 days.

B. 47.9 days.

C. 78.5 days.

Working Capital Management

Firm J's operating cycle is 38 days. Firm K's operating cycle is longer at 42 days but its cash conversion cycle is shorter than that of Firm J. We can conclude that:

A. Firm J has better inventory management.

B. Firm K has better receivables management.

C. Firm K has lower payables turnover.

40- 1

-3

CFA Curriculum Vol. 4, R.39, Q.6, p. 223

1) Suppose a company uses trade credit with the terms of 2/10, net 50. If the company pays its account on the 50th day, the effective borrowing cost of skipping the discount on day 10 is *closest* to:

A. 14.9%.

B. 15.0%.

C. 20.2%.

Additional Problems

4) Sales costs and expenses for Timer, Inc.::

Sales	1 million units
Sales price/unit	€85
Variable cost/unit	€45
Fixed operating cost	€10 million
Fixed interest cost	€10 million

Timer's degree of financial leverage is *closest* to:

A. 1.3.

B. 1.5.

C. 2.0.

-2

Additional Problems

3) Currently a company has:

EPS = $3.00

Share price = $40

Shares outstanding = 1,000,000

Tax rate = 40%

The new EPS if the company borrows at 10% to finance the repurchase of 50,000 shares is *closest* to:

A. $3.02.

B. $3.03.

C. $3.04.

-3

STUDY SESSION 11 ANSWERS

Reading	Slide Number	Answer
37	10	B
39	40	C

Additional Problems

1. C

2. C

3. B

4. B

Study Session 12

Portfolio Management

LOS 40.c Describe
CFAI p. 242, Schweser p. 114

Portfolio Management:
An Overview

Pensions

Defined Contribution Plan

- Employer contributes specified sum each period
- No guarantee of future benefits
- *Employee* bears investment risk

Defined Benefit Plan

- Employer promises specific payment stream beginning at retirement
- Contributions based on years of service, compensation at/near retirement
- *Employer* bears investment risk
- Separate legal entity manages plan assets

© Kaplan, Inc.

4

CFA Curriculum Vol. 4,
R.40, Q.5, p. 265

Portfolio Management:
An Overview

Which of the following institutional investors will *most likely* have the longest time horizon?

A. Defined benefit plan.

B. University endowment.

C. Life insurance company.

5 – 1

LOS 40.d Describe
CFAI p. 248, Schweser p. 115

Portfolio Management:
An Overview

Portfolio Management Process

1. Planning

- Understand client needs and constraints
- Write an Investment Policy Statement (IPS)
- Develop an investment strategy consistent with the IPS
- Specify performance benchmark

© Kaplan, Inc.

6

LOS 40.d Describe
CFAI p. 248, Schweser p. 115

Portfolio Management:
An Overview

Portfolio Management Process

2. Execution

- Analyze risk and return characteristics of asset classes
- Analyze market conditions to identify attractive asset classes
- Identify attractive securities within asset classes
- Portfolio construction: Target/strategic asset allocations, individual securities weightings, risk management

© Kaplan, Inc.

7

Portfolio Management Process

3. Feedback

- Monitor and update investor's needs
- Monitor and update market conditions
- Rebalance portfolio as needed
- Measure and report performance

Additional Learning Outcomes

LOS 40.b: characteristics and needs of different types of investors

LOS 40.e: mutual funds and other pooled investments

Portfolio Management

41. Risk Management: An Introduction

KAPLAN UNIVERSITY   SCHOOL OF PROFESSIONAL AND CONTINUING EDUCATION | SCHWESER

Risk Management

Objectives of risk management:

- Identify organization's risk tolerance
- Identify and measure risks faced
- Modify and monitor risks

Risk management does not seek to avoid or minimize risk, but to identify which risks an organization is best able to take on.

Risk Management Framework

- Establish risk governance policies and processes
- Determine organization's risk tolerance
- Identify and measure risks
- Manage or mitigate risks
- Monitor risk exposures
- Communicate across organization
- Perform strategic risk analysis

© Kaplan, Inc.

12

Risk Governance

Senior management determines the organization's risk tolerance, risk exposure strategy, and framework for oversight

Risk tolerance depends on business expertise, ability to respond to events, financial strength, and regulatory environment

Risk management committee identifies risks that should be pursued, limited, or avoided

© Kaplan, Inc.

13

Risk Budgeting

Allocate the organization's desired amount of overall risk exposure among assets or investments, based on:

- Organization's goals and risk tolerance
- Risk characteristics of assets or investments

Risk budget may be a single metric such as VaR, portfolio beta, or portfolio duration

© Kaplan, Inc.

14

Financial Sources of Risk

Credit risk: Counterparties might not fulfill obligations

Liquidity risk: May receive less than fair value when selling an asset

Market risk: Uncertainty about asset prices and interest rates

© Kaplan, Inc.

15

LOS 41.f Identify/Describe
CFAI p. 286, Schweser p. 126

Risk Management:
An Introduction

Non-Financial Sources of Risk

Operational risk: Human error, faulty processes

Solvency risk: Running out of cash

Regulatory risk: Regulations impose costs or restrict activities

Political/government/tax risk: Government actions other than regulations

Legal risk: Exposure to lawsuits

© Kaplan, Inc.   16

LOS 41.f Identify/Describe
CFAI p. 286, Schweser p. 126

Risk Management:
An Introduction

Non-Financial Sources of Risk

Model risk: Incorrect asset valuations

Tail risk: Underestimating probability of extreme outcomes (for example by incorrectly assuming a normal distribution)

Accounting risk: Policies and estimates may be judged to be incorrect

© Kaplan, Inc.   17

LOS 41.g Describe
CFAI p. 296, Schweser p. 127

Risk Management:
An Introduction

Measuring Risk Exposure

Risk measures include:

Standard deviation: dispersion of outcomes

Beta: sensitivity to equity market

Duration: sensitivity to interest rates

Risk assessment methods:

Stress testing estimates the effects of changes in a single variable

Scenario analysis estimates the effects of simultaneous changes in multiple variables

© Kaplan, Inc.   18

LOS 41.g Describe
CFAI p. 296, Schweser p. 127

Risk Management:
An Introduction

Measuring Risk Exposure

Measures of tail risk:

Value-at-Risk (VaR): Minimum loss over a period with a specific probability

One-month VaR of $1 million with 5% probability means loss will exceed $1 million 5% of the time

Conditional VaR: Expected value of a loss, given that the loss is greater than the minimum loss

© Kaplan, Inc.   19

Derivatives Risk Measures

Delta: Sensitivity of derivative value to price of underlying asset

Gamma: Sensitivity of delta to changes in price of underlying asset

Vega: Sensitivity of derivative value to volatility of underlying asset

Rho: Sensitivity of derivative value to changes in risk-free rate

© Kaplan, Inc.

20

Modifying Risk Exposure

Management may choose to *accept, avoid, prevent, transfer,* or *shift* a particular risk

Accept (*self-insurance*) and bear a risk efficiently, for example through diversification

Avoid by not engaging in activities that expose the organization to a risk

Prevent, for example with stronger security

Transfer to another party (e.g., insurance)

Shift by changing the distribution of outcomes, typically with derivatives

© Kaplan, Inc.

21

Portfolio Management

Portfolio Management

42. Portfolio Risk and Return: Part I

KAPLAN UNIVERSITY SCHOOL OF PROFESSIONAL AND CONTINUING EDUCATION | SCHWESER

Return Measures

Holding Period (Total) Return

$$\frac{\text{End-of-period value}}{\text{Beginning-of-period value}} - 1$$

Average Return

$$\frac{R_1 + R_2 + R_3 + \ldots\ldots + R_n}{n}$$

© Kaplan, Inc.

23

Slide 24

Return Measures

Geometric Mean Return

$$\sqrt[n]{(1+R_1)(1+R_2)(1+R_3)\ldots\ldots(1+R_n)}-1$$

Slide 25-4

Invest $1,000 in an account at t = 0

Value at end of Year 1 is $1,200, investor **adds $800**.

Value at end of Year 2 is $2,200.

Calculate the annual TWR and MWR.

(1) TWR =

(2) MWR =

Slide 26

Return Measures

Gross return: Return before management fees

Net return: Return after management fees

After-tax return: After deducting tax liability

Real return: After adjusting for inflation

Leveraged return: Return on cash investment

Slide 27-3

An investor buys 500 shares at $35 with 50% margin. After one year, the shares are sold for $50. The investor is subject to a 15% tax on gains, and inflation over the year was 4%. Ignoring interest and commissions, the investor's real after-tax leveraged return is:

Slide 28

Major Asset Classes

Asset Class	Annual Returns	Standard Deviation
Small-cap	11.7%	33.0%
Large-cap	9.6%	20.9%
LT Corporate Bonds	5.9%	8.4%
LT Treasury Bonds	5.7%	9.4%
Treasury Bills	3.7%	3.1%
Inflation	3.0%	4.2%

Source: 2009 Ibbotson SBBI Classic Yearbook

© Kaplan, Inc.

28

Slide 29

Mean, Variance, Covariance

Year	Asset A	Asset B
1	+0.05	+0.07
2	−0.02	−0.04
3	+0.12	+0.18

Mean return, Asset A $= (5 − 2 + 12) / 3 = 5\%$

Mean return, Asset B $= (7 − 4 + 18) / 3 = 7\%$

© Kaplan, Inc.

29

Slide 30

Mean, Variance, Covariance, Correlation

Year	Asset A	Asset B
1	+0.05	+0.07
2	−0.02	−0.04
3	+0.12	+0.18
Mean	0.05	0.07

$Var_A = \dfrac{(5−5)^2 + (−2−5)^2 + (12−5)^2}{3−1} = 49 \,(0.0049)$ Std. Dev. $= 7\%$

$Var_B = \dfrac{(7−7)^2 + (−4−7)^2 + (18−7)^2}{3−1} = 121 \,(0.0121)$ Std. Dev. $= 11\%$

© Kaplan, Inc.

30

Slide 31

Mean, Variance, Covariance, Correlation

Year	Asset A	Asset B
1	+0.05	+0.07
2	−0.02	−0.04
3	+0.12	+0.18
Mean	0.05	0.07

Covariance of returns for Assets A and B:

$\dfrac{(5−5)(7−7) + (−2−5)(−4−7) + (12−5)(18−7)}{3−1} = 77 = 0.0077$

© Kaplan, Inc.

31

Mean, Variance, Covariance, Correlation

$Cov_{AB} = 0.0077$; $\sigma_A = 0.07$; $\sigma_B = 0.11$

$$\rho_{A,B} = \frac{Cov_{A,B}}{\sigma_A \sigma_B}$$

$$\rho_{A,B} = \frac{0.0077}{(0.07)(0.11)} = 1$$

The returns on Assets A and B are perfectly positively correlated in this example.

© Kaplan, Inc.

32

Risk Aversion

Risk aversion means investors prefer less risk to more risk

When two investments have equal expected returns, investors prefer the one with lower risk

When two investments have equal risk, investors prefer the one with higher expected return

Investors do not *minimize* risk. It's a trade-off!

© Kaplan, Inc.

33

Abner is risk averse. Which of the following statements is *most likely* correct?

A. He will choose relatively safe investments.

B. He may hold some very risky investments.

C. His risk tolerance is relatively low.

© Kaplan, Inc.

34 – 1

Portfolio Standard Deviation

$$Var(R_p) = \sigma_A^2 w_A^2 + \sigma_B^2 w_B^2 + 2w_A w_B Cov_{AB}$$

$$Note: Cov_{AB} = \rho_{AB}\sigma_A \sigma_B$$

$$Var(R_p) = \sigma_A^2 w_A^2 + \sigma_B^2 w_B^2 + 2w_A w_B \rho_{AB}\sigma_A \sigma_B$$

© Kaplan, Inc.

35

Portfolio Management

40. Portfolio Management: An Overview

Study Session 12
Portfolio Management

40. Portfolio Management: An Overview
41. Risk Management: An Introduction
42. Portfolio Risk and Return: Part I
43. Portfolio Risk and Return: Part II
44. Basics of Portfolio Planning and Construction

Which of the following institutions will *on average*
have the greatest need for liquidity?

A. Banks.

B. Investment companies.

C. Non-life insurance companies.

3 - 1

The Portfolio Perspective

Evaluate investments based on their
contribution to risk and return of an
investor's overall portfolio (not in isolation)

Adding a risky asset can actually reduce
portfolio risk

Diversification ratio =

$$\frac{\text{std. dev. of equal-weighted portfolio's returns}}{\text{average std. dev. of returns on portfolio assets}}$$

2

LOS 42.f Describe
CFAI p. 356, Schweser p. 144

Correlation and Risk Reduction

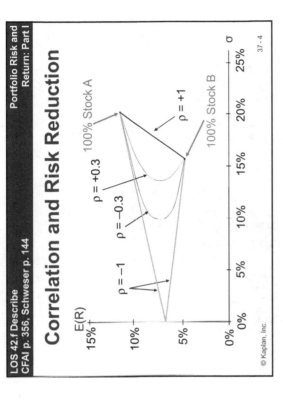

37 - 4

A portfolio is 30% invested in stocks, $\sigma = 20\%$, with the remainder in bonds, $\sigma = 12\%$. The correlation of bond returns with stock returns is 0.60. What is the standard deviation of portfolio returns?

36 - 2

LOS 42.g Describe/Interpret
CFAI p. 362, Schweser p. 146

Minimum Variance Frontier and Efficient Frontier

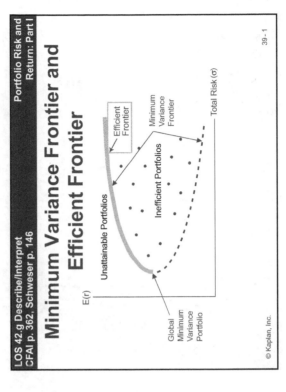

39 - 1

An asset has correlation with a portfolio's return that is less than 1 but has the same standard deviation of returns as the portfolio. What is the *most likely* effect of adding some of this asset to the portfolio have on the portfolio risk? Portfolio risk:

A. will decrease.
B. will increase.
C. may increase or decrease depending on the individual securities mix in the portfolio.

38 - 1

LOS 42.h Discuss
CFAI p. 368, Schweser p. 147

Portfolio Risk and Return: Part I

Adding a Risk-Free Asset

When a risk-free asset is combined with a risky asset or portfolio, the risk/return of each possible combination is referred to as the **Capital Allocation Line (CAL)**

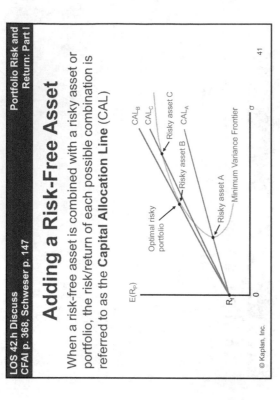

41

Portfolio Risk and Return: Part I

Which of the following portfolios is *least likely* on the efficient frontier?

Portfolio	Expected Return	Std. Dev.
A.	10%	12%
B.	12%	16%
C.	14%	15%

40 – 2

CFA Curriculum Vol. 4,
R.42, Q.37, p. 382

Portfolio Risk and Return: Part I

The set of portfolios on the minimum-variance frontier that dominates all sets of portfolios below the global minimum-variance portfolio is the:

A. capital allocation line.

B. Markowitz efficient frontier.

C. set of optimal risky portfolios.

43 – 1

LOS 42.h Discuss
CFAI p. 368, Schweser p. 147

Portfolio Risk and Return: Part I

Investor's Optimal Portfolio

Investor A is more risk averse than Investor B (steeper indifference curves).

Investor A selects a less-risky optimal portfolio (portfolio that maximizes investor's expected utility).

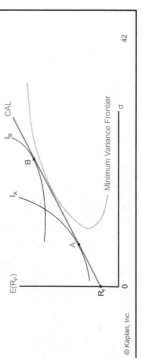

42

Portfolio Management

Portfolio Management

43. Portfolio Risk and Return: Part II

KAPLAN UNIVERSITY SCHOOL OF PROFESSIONAL AND CONTINUING EDUCATION | SCHWESER

LOS 43.a Describe
CFAI p. 388, Schweser p. 158

Portfolio Risk and Return: Part II

Combining Risk-free and Risky Assets

Portfolio expected return = $W_{risky} R_p + W_{Rf} R_f$

Portfolio std. dev. = $W_{risky} \sigma_p$

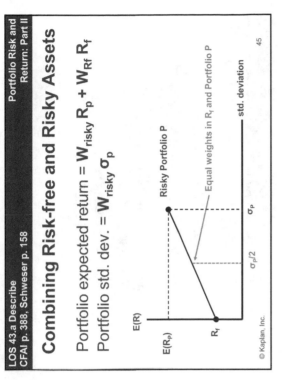

© Kaplan, Inc.   45

LOS 43.b Explain
CFAI p. 388, Schweser p. 159

Portfolio Risk and Return: Part II

Capital Allocation Line

The risk/return combinations resulting from combining a risk-free asset with a portfolio of risky assets

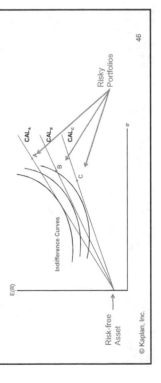

© Kaplan, Inc.   46

LOS 43.b Explain
CFAI p. 388, Schweser p. 159

Portfolio Risk and Return: Part II

Capital Market Line

With homogeneous expectations, all investors have the same optimal risky portfolio

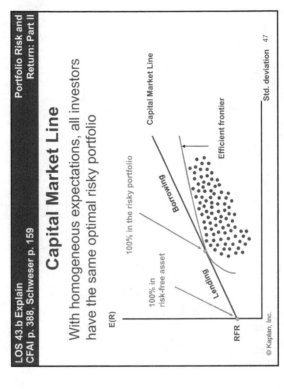

© Kaplan, Inc.   47

Diversification and the Reduction of Unsystematic Risk

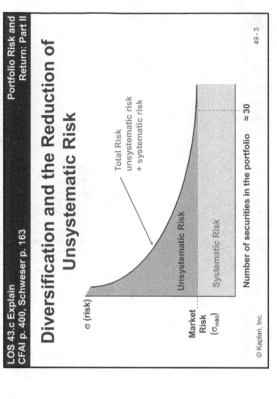

49 - 3

© Kaplan, Inc.

Systematic and Unsystematic Risk

Systematic risk (market risk)

- Caused by macro factors: Interest rates, GDP growth, supply shocks
- Measured by covariance of returns with returns on the market portfolio

Unsystematic risk (firm-specific risk)

- Can be reduced/eliminated by holding well-diversified portfolios

CAPM: Only systematic (market) risk is rewarded with higher expected returns

48

© Kaplan, Inc.

Returns Generating Models

Multi-factor Models

$$E[R_j] - R_f = \beta_{i,1} E[F_1] + \beta_{i,2} E[F_2] + \ldots + \beta_{i,K} E[F_K]$$

The factors (F's) are the expected values of each risk factor

The betas ($\beta_{i,k}$) are the asset's factor sensitivities or factor loadings for each risk factor

51

© Kaplan, Inc.

Returns Generating Models

The Market Model

$$R_i = \alpha_i + \beta_i R_m + e_i$$

- The market model has a single risk factor, the return on the market
- The asset's beta (β_i) is the sensitivity of its returns to this risk factor
- Asset returns are a linear function of market returns

50

© Kaplan, Inc.

Returns Generating Models

Multi-factor Models

$$E[R_i] - R_f = \beta_{i,1} E[F_1] + \beta_{i,2} E[F_2] + \ldots + \beta_{i,K} E[F_K]$$

Risk factors (F) of three types:

1. **Macroeconomic factors** e.g., GDP growth, inflation, consumer confidence

2. **Fundamental factors** e.g., earnings, earnings growth, firm size, research expenditures

3. **Statistical factors**, no basis in finance theory

© Kaplan, Inc.

52

Returns Generating Models

Fama and French 3-factor Model

Risk factors are:

1. Firm size

2. Book-to-market ratio

3. Excess return on the market portfolio

Carhart added a fourth factor, momentum

These models explain U.S. equity returns better than the market (single-index) model

© Kaplan, Inc.

53

Calculating Beta

In the market model, beta is often estimated as the slope of a regression of asset returns on market returns: **Characteristic Line**

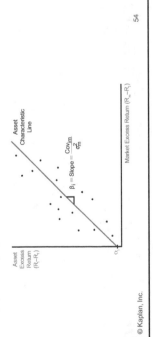

© Kaplan, Inc.

54

Calculating Beta

$$Beta_i = \frac{Cov_{i,mkt}}{\sigma_{mkt}^2} \qquad Beta_{Portfolio} = \sum_{i=1}^{n} w_i Beta_i$$

$$Beta_i = \rho_{i,mkt}\left(\frac{\sigma_i}{\sigma_{mkt}}\right) = \frac{Cov_{i,mkt}}{\sigma_i \sigma_{mkt}}\left(\frac{\sigma_i}{\sigma_{mkt}}\right) = \frac{Cov_{i,mkt}}{\sigma_{mkt}^2}$$

$$Beta_{mkt} = \rho_{mkt,mkt}\left(\frac{\sigma_{mkt}}{\sigma_{mkt}}\right) = 1$$

© Kaplan, Inc.

55

LOS 43.f Explain
CFAI p. 409, Schweser p. 168

The Capital Asset Pricing Model

SML equation:

$$E(R_i) = RFR + \beta_i \underbrace{[E(R_{mkt}) - RFR]}_{\text{Market risk premium}}$$

Beta is a measure of systematic risk

Beta is the standardized covariance of an asset's returns with returns on the market portfolio

$$\beta_i = \frac{Cov_{i,mkt}}{\sigma^2_{mkt}}$$

© Kaplan, Inc.

57

LOS 43.f Explain
CFAI p. 409, Schweser p. 168

Security Market Line (SML)

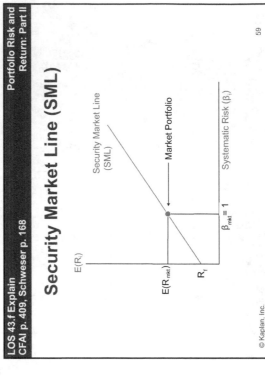

© Kaplan, Inc.

59

LOS 43.f Explain
CFAI p. 409, Schweser p. 168

Assumptions of Capital Market Theory

- Investors use **mean-variance** framework
- **Unlimited lending and borrowing** at R_f
- Homogeneous **expectations**
- **One-period** time horizon
- **Divisible** assets
- **Frictionless** markets
- No inflation and **unchanging interest rates**
- Capital markets are in **equilibrium, investors are price takers**

© Kaplan, Inc.

56

LOS 43.f Explain
CFAI p. 409, Schweser p. 168

Capital Asset Pricing Model (CAPM)

CAPM: The expected return on an asset based only on the asset's systematic risk or beta

CAPM can also be used to determine the required return on an asset based on the asset's systematic risk (beta)

Required return and expected return are the same in equilibrium

© Kaplan, Inc.

58

CAPM Expected Returns Example

A stock has a beta of 1.2, the expected return on the market is 8%, and the risk-free rate is 2%. What is the stock's expected return?

Risk-free
Rate

Market
Risk
Premium

Beta

Expected return = 2% + 1.2 (8% − 2%) = 9.2%

In equilibrium the expected return and the required return in the market are equal

© Kaplan, Inc.

60

CAPM Applications

Calculating risk-adjusted return measures

Treynor measure =
$(R_P − R_f)/\beta_P$

slope = Treynor measure for Portfolio P

Jensen's alpha

Compare to the
slope of the SML

Jensen's alpha = $R_P − [R_f + \beta_P (R_M − R_f)]$

Jensen's alpha is the % return above the equilibrium return for a portfolio with beta = β_P

© Kaplan, Inc.

62 - 3

CAPM Applications

Calculating risk-adjusted return measures

CAL slope = $\dfrac{R_{p2} − R_f}{\sigma_{p2}}$

CML slope = $\dfrac{R_M − R_f}{\sigma_M} = \dfrac{R_{p1} − R_f}{\sigma_{P1}}$

Sharpe ratio of P2 is slope of the CAL

Compare to the slope of the CML

The M² measure for P2 is $(R_{P2} − R_f) (\sigma_M/\sigma_{P2}) − (R_M − R_f)$

M² is the extra % return for a (leveraged) portfolio with same (total) risk as the market portfolio

© Kaplan, Inc.

61 - 4

Forecast Returns and the CAPM Example

An analyst has forecast the following for three stocks. $R_f = 7\%$ $E(R_{mkt}) = 15\%$

Stock	Price Today	E (price) in 1 year	E (dividend) in 1 year	Beta
A	$25	$27	$1.00	1.0
B	40	45	2.00	0.8
C	15	17	0.50	1.2

Are these stocks overpriced, underpriced, or at their equilibrium prices? Show where they plot on the SML graph.

© Kaplan, Inc.

63

Slide 64-4

Forecast Returns and the CAPM Example

Stock	Price Today	E (price) in 1 year	E (dividend) in 1 year	Beta
A	$25	$27	$1.00	1.0
B	40	45	2.00	0.8
C	15	17	0.50	1.2

$R_f = 7\%$ $E[R_{mkt}] = 15\%$

Stock	Forecast Return	Required Return
A	(27 – 25 + 1) / 25 = 12.0%	0.07 + 1.0(0.15 – 0.07) = 15.0%
B	(45 – 40 + 2) / 40 = 17.5%	0.07 + 0.8(0.15 – 0.07) = 13.4%
C	(17 – 15 + 0.50) / 15 = 16.6%	0.07 + 1.2(0.15 – 0.07) = 16.6%

R_f MRP

© Kaplan, Inc.   64-4

Slide 65-5

Forecast Returns and the CAPM Example

When securities are priced at equilibrium values, they plot on the SML

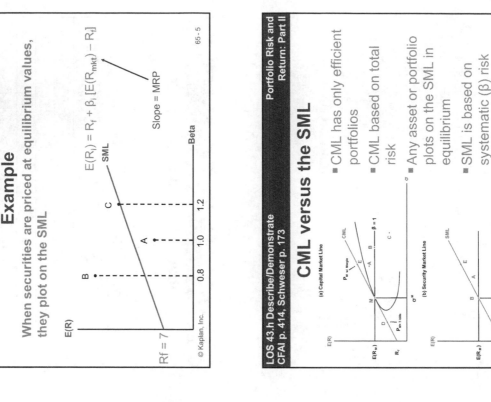

$E(R_i) = R_f + \beta_i \, [E(R_{mkt}) - R_f]$

Slope = MRP

E(R)   Rf = 7   SML   Beta   0.8   1.0   1.2   B   A   C

© Kaplan, Inc.   65-5

Slide 67-4

CML versus the SML

- CML has only efficient portfolios
- CML based on total risk
- Any asset or portfolio plots on the SML in equilibrium
- SML is based on systematic (β) risk

(a) Capital Market Line

(b) Security Market Line

© Kaplan, Inc.   67-4

Slide 66

Forecast Returns and the CAPM

Stock	Forecast Return	Required Return
A	12.0%	15.0%
B	17.5%	13.4%
C	16.6%	16.6%

Stock A is overvalued (sell it or sell it short)

Stock B is undervalued (buy it)

Stock C is properly valued (indifferent)

© Kaplan, Inc.   66

Portfolio Management

44. Basics of Portfolio Planning and Construction

KAPLAN UNIVERSITY · SCHOOL OF PROFESSIONAL AND CONTINUING EDUCATION | SCHWESER

© Kaplan, Inc.

$E[R_{mkt}] = 15\%$ $RFR = 8\%$ Stock X's beta = 1.25
Forecast $R_{Stock\ X} = 17\%$

Using these data and the CAPM, which of the following statements about Stock X is true based on the analyst forecast? Stock X is:

A. overvalued by 1.75 percentage points.
B. properly valued.
C. undervalued by 0.25 percentage points.

68-2

© Kaplan, Inc.

LOS 44.a Describe
CFAI p. 440, Schweser p. 184

Investment Policy Statement

- Identifies client objectives and constraints
- Clear statement of client risk tolerance
- Imposes investment discipline on both client and manager
- Identifies risks
- Identifies a benchmark portfolio consistent with client preferences

70

© Kaplan, Inc.

LOS 44.b Describe
CFAI p. 441; Schweser p. 184

Major Components of an IPS

- Description of client circumstances
- Purpose of the IPS
- Duties and responsibilities of all parties
- Procedures to update IPS, resolve problems
- Investment objectives and constraints
- Investment guidelines
- Evaluation of performance, benchmark
- Appendices: Strategic asset allocation, permitted deviations, rebalancing procedures

71

© Kaplan, Inc.

Investment Objectives

Investment objectives should include both risk and return objectives because of the trade-off between risk and expected return

Factors affecting investor risk tolerance:

- Psychological factors
- Personal factors: Age, family situation, existing wealth, insurance coverage, cash reserves, income

© Kaplan, Inc.

72

Risk Tolerance

Ability to bear risk depends on investment horizon, insurance, income, wealth, financial responsibilities

Willingness to bear risk depends on attitudes and beliefs about investment risk

Willingness > ability: Advisor should go with ability

Ability > willingness: Educate the investor about investment risk, do not attempt to change personality/psychological characteristics

© Kaplan, Inc.

73

Investment Constraints

Liquidity: The potential need for cash

Legal and regulatory: Applies to institutional investors, but also affects individual investors (e.g., IRA accounts)

Time horizon: The time until the proceeds of the investment will be required

Tax concerns: Is the account taxable, tax-deferred, or tax-exempt?

Unique circumstances: Anything that does not fit into the above categories

© Kaplan, Inc.

74

Strategic Asset Allocation

- Based on risk, returns, and correlations of asset classes
- Correlations of returns of assets within an asset class should be relatively high
- Correlations of returns between asset classes should be low

© Kaplan, Inc.

75

Strategic Asset Allocation Example

Cash	2%
Large-cap U.S. Equity	13%
Mid- Small-cap U.S. Equity	8%
International Developed Equity	12%
Emerging Markets Equity	9%
High-yield Bonds	7%
U.S. Bonds	18%
International Bonds	14%
Real Estate	11%
Hedge Funds	6%

© Kaplan, Inc.

76

Portfolio Construction

- Use risk, return, and correlations of asset classes to construct an **efficient frontier**
- Use objectives and constraints from IPS to select an optimal portfolio (**strategic allocation**)
  - **Tactical asset allocation** (deviations from strategic allocation) and security selection as permitted and appropriate
  - **Risk budgeting** allocates permitted risk to the three sources: strategic allocation, tactical allocation, and security selection

© Kaplan, Inc.

77

Additional Problems

KAPLAN UNIVERSITY SCHOOL OF PROFESSIONAL AND CONTINUING EDUCATION SCHWESER

Additional Problems

1) The optimal risky portfolio has an expected return of 10% and standard deviation of 19%. If a risk-free asset is available, an investor whose risk tolerance implies an optimal portfolio with a 24% standard deviation should:

A. invest 100% in the risky portfolio.

B. purchase some of the risk-free asset for his portfolio.

C. borrow at the risk-free rate.

© Kaplan, Inc.

- 3

**CFA Curriculum Vol. 4,
R.42, Q.19, p. 379**

3) With respect to an investor's utility function expressed as: $U = E(r) - \frac{1}{2}A\sigma^2$, which of the following values for the measure of risk aversion indicates the *least* amount of risk aversion?

A. –4.

B. 0.

C. 4.

- 2

Additional Problems

2) Relatively steep indifference curves for expected return and standard deviation of returns are *most likely* associated with which type of investor?

A. Highly risk-averse.

B. Risk-neutral.

C. Highly risk-tolerant investor.

- 2

Additional Problems

4) The *most appropriate* measure of performance for a concentrated portfolio is:

A. M-squared.

B. Treynor's ratio.

C. Jensen's alpha.

- 3

STUDY SESSION 12 ANSWERS

Reading	Slide Number	Answer
40	3	A
40	5	B
42	25 (1)	14.89%
42	25 (2)	13.623%
42	27	66.2%
42	34	B
42	36	12.9%
42	38	A
42	40	B
42	43	B
43	68	C

Additional Problems

1. C

2. A

3. A

4. A

Study Session 13

Equity: Market Organization, Market Indices, and Market Efficiency

Market Organization, Market Indices, and Market Efficiency

45. Market Organization and Structure

KAPLAN UNIVERSITY SCHOOL OF PROFESSIONAL AND CONTINUING EDUCATION | SCHWESER

Study Session 13

Market Organization, Market Indices, and Market Efficiency

45. Market Organization and Structure
46. Security Market Indices
47. Market Efficiency

KAPLAN UNIVERSITY SCHOOL OF PROFESSIONAL AND CONTINUING EDUCATION | SCHWESER

Market Organization and Structure

LOS 45.d Describe
CFAI p. 28, Schweser p. 202

Financial Intermediary Roles

Securitizers, depository institutions: Sell interests in a diversified pool of assets

Insurance companies: Manage a diversified pool of risks

Clearinghouses: Reduce counterparty risk and promote market integrity

© Kaplan, Inc.

3

Market Organization and Structure

LOS 45.d Describe
CFAI p. 28, Schweser p. 202

Financial Intermediary Roles

Brokers, exchanges: Connect buyers, sellers of same security at same location and time

Dealers: Act as principal, trades for own account

Arbitrageurs: Transact with buyers, sellers of same security at same time but in different markets

© Kaplan, Inc.

2

Selling Short

1. Investor **borrows stock** and sells it

2. Later, **repurchases the stock** and returns it to the lender (covers the short position)

3. Short seller's **profit (loss)** is the original selling price minus the repurchase price (interest, commissions)

Rules of short selling:

- Short sellers **pay all dividends** to the lender
- Short seller **deposits margin/collateral**

  Sell high and buy low

© Kaplan, Inc.

4

Buying Stock on Margin

Margin: Borrow part of the money to buy stock

- Brokers hold the stock as collateral
- **Margin requirement:** Required equity %
- **Maintenance margin:** Minimum equity %

$$\text{Equity percentage} = \frac{\text{stock value} - \text{loan}}{\text{stock value}}$$

© Kaplan, Inc.

5

Example: Return on Margin Position

- An investor buys 1,000 shares of a stock on margin at a price of $60 per share

- Initial margin requirement is 50% and margin loan rate is 2%

- Stock pays annual dividend of $0.40 per share

- Commission is $0.01 per share on purchase, sale

- One year later, investor sells stock at $66 per share

- **Calculate** the leverage ratio

- **Calculate** investor's return on the margin position

© Kaplan, Inc.

6

Return on Margin Position

Leverage ratio

= 1 / minimum margin requirement = 1 / 0.50 = **2.0**

Ignoring transactions costs, dividends, and interest, a price return of 10% on the stock would result in a return of 2 × 10% = 20% on invested cash

© Kaplan, Inc.

7

Market Organization and Structure

Margin Call Price Calculation

Investor buys a stock on margin at a price of $70
Initial margin requirement = 40%
Maintenance margin = 25%
Below what stock price will the investor receive a margin call?

- Loan amount is $1 - 40\% = 60\%$ of $70 = $42/sh.
- When equity is 25%, loan amount must be 75%
- $42 = 0.75 \times$ margin call price
- Margin call below = $42 / 0.75 = $56/sh.

© Kaplan, Inc.

9 - 4

Market Organization and Structure

Quote-driven (Dealer) Markets

Limit sell orders
17.96 × 300	⎤ Behind or away from the market
17.88 × 500	⎦
17.85 × 200	← Best offer

"The market" 17.75 bid, 17.85 offer

Limit buy orders
17.75 × 400	← Best bid
17.70 × 300	⎤ Behind or away from the market
17.67 × 100	⎦

Sale at 17.75 or buy at 17.85 "takes the market"
Bid or offer between 17.75 and 17.85 "makes a new market"

© Kaplan, Inc.

11

Market Organization and Structure

Return on Margin Position

Investor equity = 0.50 × $60 × 1,000 =	$30,000
+ Commission on purchase = $0.01 × 1,000 =	$10
Total investment =	**$30,010**
Sale proceeds = $66 × 1,000 =	$66,000
+ Dividends = 1,000 × $0.40 =	$400
– Interest on loan = $30,000 × 2% =	$600
– Commission on sale = $0.01 × 1,000 =	$10
– Repay loan	$30,000
Total Proceeds =	**$35,790**

Return = ($35,790 / $30,010) − 1 = 19.26%

© Kaplan, Inc.

8

Market Organization and Structure

Trading Instructions

Execution: How to trade

Market orders: Best price available

Limit orders: Specified price or better

Validity: When to trade

Good-til-cancelled, day orders, stop orders

Clearing: How to settle trade

Custodian, long or short

© Kaplan, Inc.

10

Slide 12

Types of Orders

Market order:

Immediate execution, best available price

Limit order:

- Buy at limit price or lower
- Sell at limit price or higher

Stop (loss) order:

A trade at the stop price activates a market order

- Buy if stock goes up to stop price
- Sell if stock goes down to stop price

Can have stop limit order, stop triggers a limit order

© Kaplan, Inc.

12

Slide 13-2

A trader who owns a stock that is trading at 48 and would like to buy more shares if it increases in value to 52 should enter a:

A. limit buy order at 52.

B. market buy order at 52.

C. stop buy order at 52.

© Kaplan, Inc.

13 - 2

Slide 14

Market Structures

Quote-driven: Investors trade with dealers

Order-driven: Rules used to match buyers and sellers, price, time,

Brokered markets: Broker finds counterparty for a trade

© Kaplan, Inc.

14

Slide 15

Additional Learning Outcomes

LOS 45.a: functions of the financial system

LOS 45.b: classifications of assets and markets

LOS 45.c: securities, currencies, contracts, commodities, and real assets

LOS 45.i: primary and secondary markets

LOS 45.k: characteristics of a well-functioning financial system

LOS 45.l: objectives of market regulation

© Kaplan, Inc.

15

Market Organization, Market Indices, and Market Efficiency

46. Security Market Indices

LOS 46.a,b Describe/Calculate/Interpret   Security Market Indices
CFAI p. 78, Schweser p. 225

Security Market Indexes

Represents value/performance of an asset class, security market, or market segment over time

There are various weighting schemes for constituent securities' values/performance

Price return index only reflects changes in market prices of constituent securities

Total return index includes cash flows from the securities in the index (dividends, interest)

© Kaplan, Inc.   17

LOS 46.c Describe   Security Market Indices
CFAI p. 82, Schweser p. 226

Index Construction Decisions

What market does the index represent?

Which securities will be included?

Which weighting method will be used?

When will the index be rebalanced?

When will the index's securities be re-examined?

© Kaplan, Inc.   18

LOS 46.d Compare   Security Market Indices
CFAI p. 83, Schweser p. 226

Equal-Weighted Index

$$EWI = \frac{Ret_1 + Ret_2 + Ret_3 + \ldots + Ret_N}{N}$$

- An equal-weighted index gives the **same weight to the performance of each index stock**

  ■ Match with portfolio of equal amounts invested in each index stock

  ■ Index return is the average return on index stocks

  ■ Rebalancing—often quarterly

© Kaplan, Inc.   19

Price-Weighted Index (PWI)

$$PWI = \frac{\text{sum of stock prices}}{\text{\# stocks in index, adjusted for splits}}$$

- Match by buying an **equal number of shares** of each stock in the index

- Returns on high-price stocks have greatest effect on the index

- DJIA and Nikkei 225

© Kaplan, Inc.

20

Market-Cap Weighted Index

$$MCWI = \frac{\Sigma \ (\text{price}_{\text{today}})(\text{\# shares})}{\Sigma \ (\text{price}_{\text{base year}})(\text{\# shares})} \times \text{beg. index value}$$

- Match portfolio weights to each stock's % of total market value of index stocks

- Firms with larger market capitalizations have greater influence on the index (AAPL, XOM, MSFT)

- S&P 500, NYSE Index, and Wilshire 5000

Momentum tilt: Overpriced are over-represented, underpriced are under-represented

© Kaplan, Inc.

21

Float-adjusted Index Weights

Market float-weighted index with number of shares equal to investable shares (excludes shares of controlling investors and often those held by governments or corporations)

Free float-weighted index when shares not available to foreign investors are excluded

© Kaplan, Inc.

22

Fundamental Index Weights

Firm weight in index is % of total for all index firms:

- revenue
- earnings
- book value
- cash flow
- dividends

- Leads to a **value tilt** (e.g., book value weighted index puts more weight on firms with high book-to-market ratios)

- GDP weights are used in multi-market indexes

© Kaplan, Inc.

23

Comparing Weighting Schemes

Compared to market-cap weighted index:

Price-weighted index places more weight on high-price stocks and less on low-price stocks; stock splits change all weights (and divisor)

Equal-weighted index places more weight on small-cap stocks and less on large-cap stocks; must be rebalanced

Float-adjusted index more closely matches investable shares proportions

Fundamental-weighted index has a value tilt

© Kaplan, Inc.   24

Calculating a Price-Weighted Index

Stock	Nov. 30			Dec. 31		
	Share Price	# of Shares	Market Value	Share Price	# of Shares	Market Value
A	$20	300	$6,000	$22	300	$6,600
B	$30	200	$6,000	$27	200	$5,400
C	$40	100	$4,000	$44	100	$4,400
Total	$90		$16,000	$93		$16,400

Price-weighted index:

$90 / 3 = 30.0

$93 / 3 = 31.0

93 / 90 − 1 = +3.33%

© Kaplan, Inc.   25

Calculating a Cap-Weighted Index

Stock	Nov. 30			Dec. 31		
	Share Price	# of Shares	Market Cap	Share Price	# of Shares	Market Cap
A	$20	300	$6,000	$22	300	$6,600
B	$30	200	$6,000	$27	200	$5,400
C	$40	100	$4,000	$44	100	$4,400
Total	$90		$16,000	$93		$16,400

Beginning index value Nov. 30 = 100

New value Dec. 31 = (16,400 / 16,000) × 100 = 102.5

The total market value of all index stocks is up 2.5%

© Kaplan, Inc.   26

Calculating an Equal-Weighted Index

Stock	Initial Price	Current Price	HPR
X	$30.00	$27.00	−10%
Y	$10.00	$15.00	+50%
Z	$20.00	$22.00	+10%

$$\text{Arithmetic mean} = \frac{-10\% + 50\% + 10\%}{3} = +16.67\%$$

Initial index value = 100

Current index value = 116.67

© Kaplan, Inc.   27

Compared to a market-cap weighted index, a fundamental weighted index based on dividends will place more weight on firms with higher:

A. dividend yields.

B. dividends per share.

C. total dividend payments.

29 - 2

© Kaplan, Inc.

The type of index weighting that is *most likely* to be similar to a momentum strategy is:

A. market-cap weighting.

B. fundamental weighting.

C. equal weighting.

31 - 2

© Kaplan, Inc.

LOS 46.f Describe
CFAI p. 91, Schweser p. 232

Rebalancing and Reconstitution

Rebalancing: Updating the index weights; equal-weighted indexes are periodically rebalanced

Reconstitution: Periodically adding and deleting securities

28

© Kaplan, Inc.

LOS 46.g Describe
CFAI p. 93, Schweser p. 233

Uses of Indexes

- Reflection of market sentiment

- Performance benchmark

- Measure of market return

- Calculate beta

- Calculate expected and risk-adjusted returns

- Model portfolio for index funds

30

© Kaplan, Inc.

Market Organization, Market Indices, and Market Efficiency

47. Market Efficiency

KAPLAN UNIVERSITY   SCHOOL OF PROFESSIONAL AND CONTINUING EDUCATION | SCHWESER

LOS 47.b Distinguish
CFAI p. 119, Schweser p. 245

Market Value and Intrinsic Value

Market value: Price at which asset can be bought or sold

Intrinsic value: Value rational investors would place on an asset with full knowledge of its characteristics

If markets are not efficient, market values differ from intrinsic values in predictable ways

© Kaplan, Inc.

35

Additional Learning Outcomes

LOS 46.h: equity indices

LOS 46.i: fixed income indices

LOS 46.j: alternative investments indices

LOS 46.k: types of security market indices

© Kaplan, Inc.

32

LOS 47.a Describe
CFAI p. 117, Schweser p. 244

What are Efficient Capital Markets?

Efficient in this context means **informational efficiency**: security prices quickly and fully reflect available information in a statistical sense

Prices are efficient with respect to a particular information set if investors **cannot** use that information to **earn positive abnormal (risk-adjusted) returns on average** (i.e., cannot "beat the market")

© Kaplan, Inc.

34

LOS 47.c Explain
CFAI p. 120, Schweser p. 245   **Market Efficiency**

Factors Affecting Market Efficiency

- Number of market participants

- Availability of information

- Impediments to trading

- Transactions and information costs

© Kaplan, Inc.   36

LOS 47.d Contrast
CFAI p. 124, Schweser p. 246   **Market Efficiency**

Forms of the EMH

Efficient with respect to:

Strong form

Semistrong form

Weak form

Private information
Public information
Market information

© Kaplan, Inc.   37 – 3

LOS 47.e Explain
CFAI p. 128, Schweser p. 247   **Market Efficiency**

Implications for Active Management

If markets are <u>weak-form efficient</u>, technical analysis is useless

If markets are <u>semi-strong-form efficient</u>, both fundamental and technical analysis are useless

Evidence supports both weak-form and semi-strong-form efficiency

Markets are not strong-form efficient

© Kaplan, Inc.   38

LOS 47.f Describe
CFAI p. 129, Schweser p. 248   **Market Efficiency**

Market Anomalies

Observed market inefficiencies – evidence of predictable risk-adjusted returns

Calendar effects: January, weekend, holiday

Overreaction: Prices overreact to news

Momentum: Trends in stock returns

Size effect: Small-cap stocks outperform

Value effect: Low P/E, P/B, or P/S, high div. yield

Closed-end funds: Selling at a discount to NAV

Earnings surprises: Slow adjustment

IPOs: Initial overreaction, LT underperformance

© Kaplan, Inc.   39

Explaining Anomalies

Data mining: When many strategies are tested, some will "work" just by chance (type 1 error)

Much anomaly evidence appears to result from **estimation method** for expected returns

Many anomalies are not profitable after **transaction costs**

Some strategies do not work **after being identified**

Some strategies work **only for some time periods**

Some anomalies have **no economic basis**

40

Behavioral Finance

Investors have cognitive biases and behave in ways that are not rational

Researchers have tried to explain anomalies with:
Loss aversion: Risk aversion is asymmetrical, investors dislike losses more than they like gains
Overconfidence: Investors overestimate their ability to value securities
Herding: Investors tend to mimic actions of other investors

Markets can still be efficient even if investors exhibit irrational behavior

41

Additional Problems

1) If a researcher conducting empirical tests of a trading strategy using time series of returns finds statistically significant abnormal returns, then the researcher has *most likely* found:

A. a market anomaly.

B. evidence of market inefficiency.

C. a strategy to produce future abnormal returns.

- 3

STUDY SESSION 13 ANSWERS

Reading	Slide Number	Answer
45	13	C
46	29	A
46	31	A

Additional Problem

1. A

Study Session 14

Equity Analysis and Valuation

Study Session 14
Equity Analysis and Valuation

48. Overview of Equity Securities
49. Introduction to Industry and Company Analysis
50. Equity Valuation: Concepts and Basic Tools

KAPLAN UNIVERSITY | SCHOOL OF PROFESSIONAL AND CONTINUING EDUCATION | SCHWESER

Equity Analysis and Valuation

48. Overview of Equity Securities

KAPLAN UNIVERSITY | SCHOOL OF PROFESSIONAL AND CONTINUING EDUCATION | SCHWESER

Common Stock (Ordinary Shares)

Common shareholders have a residual claim to firm assets

Common shareholders vote for board members and on some issues (in person or by **proxy**)

Different classes of common shares can have different number of votes per share

Common stock can have a call or put feature

Statutory vs. Cumulative Voting

Consider an owner of 100 shares of common stock when 3 board members are to be elected:

Statutory (non-cumulative) voting: Shareholder can give maximum of 100 votes to each of 3 candidates

Cumulative voting: Shareholder can give maximum of 300 votes to one candidate, allows minority shareholders to gain board seats

---

Convertible Preferred Stock

Convertible preferred shares can be exchanged for a given number of common shares (i.e., at the **conversion ratio**)

Preferred dividend > common dividend

Shareholders can benefit from firm growth by converting to common

Less risky than common stock

© Kaplan, Inc.

5

Private Equity Securities

- **Venture capital** firms purchase equity early in a firm's life

- In a **leveraged buyout** (LBO), debt is used to buy all outstanding public equity

- A **management buyout** (MBO) is an LBO by the current management of the company

- **Private Investment in Public Entity** (PIPE), public firm raises equity capital though a private placement

© Kaplan, Inc.

7

Preferred Stock (Preference Shares)

- Dividends have **priority** over common stock
- Dividends are **cumulative** or **non-cumulative**
- Like common stock, they have **no maturity date**
- Typically have **no voting rights**
- Most are **non-participating**, dividend is fixed
- **Participating** preferred shares receive greater dividends if profit targets are reached
- Preferred shares can be callable or putable

© Kaplan, Inc.

4

Private Equity

Advantages compared to public equity:
- Reporting requirements less
- Better able to focus on long term
- Potentially greater return for investors if shares are sold through an initial public offering (IPO)

Disadvantages compared to public equity:
- Less liquid, not traded in public markets
- Less ability to raise capital
- Less disclosure, may weaken governance

© Kaplan, Inc.

6

LOS 48.d Describe
CFAI p. 164, Schweser p. 260

Overview of Equity Securities

Investing in Foreign Equities

<u>Buying and selling foreign shares in foreign market</u>

- Possible higher cost, may be less liquid
- Less transparency, local language and currency
- Local market procedures, settlement, clearing

<u>Buying and selling depository receipts</u>

- Claims to foreign shares deposited in domestic bank that trade like a local stock in local currency
  - Accounting standards and market procedures are those of the local market

© Kaplan, Inc.

8

LOS 48.d Describe
CFAI p. 164, Schweser p. 260

Overview of Equity Securities

Depository Receipts

Sponsored depository receipts:

- Firm is involved with issue, investor has same voting and dividend rights as foreign shareholders
- Greater firm reporting requirements (must be registered with SEC in U.S.)

Unsponsored depository receipts:

- Depository buys shares in foreign market
- Bank retains voting rights

© Kaplan, Inc.

9

LOS 48.e Compare
CFAI p. 169, Schweser p. 261

Overview of Equity Securities

Risk Characteristics of Equity

Preferred stock is **less risky** than common stock

- Fixed dividend, less uncertainty
- Receives distributions before common stock
- Claim to par value if firm is liquidated

Callable common or preferred stock is **more risky** than non-callable

Putable common or preferred stock is **less risky** than non-putable

Cumulative preferred is **less risky** than non-cumulative

© Kaplan, Inc.

10

LOS 48.g Distinguish
CFAI p. 172, Schweser p. 262

Overview of Equity Securities

Book and Market Value of Equity

Book value of equity:
Value of the firm's balance sheet assets minus liabilities

Market value of equity:
Reflects investor expectations regarding firm risk, amount and timing of future cash flows

© Kaplan, Inc.

11

When investing in unsponsored depository receipts, the voting rights to the shares in the trust belong to:

A. the depository bank.
B. the investors in the depository receipts.
C. the issuer of the shares held in the trust.

12 – 1

ROE and Cost of Equity

ROE (net income / average equity) measures the return management is generating on equity capital

Cost of equity is investors' minimum **required rate of return** on the firm's equity securities—difficult to estimate compared to required return on debt

13

From an investor's point of view, which of the following equity securities is the *least* risky?

A. Putable preference shares.
B. Callable preference shares.
C. Non-callable preference shares.

14 – 1

Additional Learning Outcomes

LOS 48.f: role of equity securities in financing a company's assets

15

Equity Investments

Equity Analysis and Valuation

49. Introduction to Industry and Company Analysis

KAPLAN UNIVERSITY | SCHOOL OF PROFESSIONAL AND CONTINUING EDUCATION | SCHWESER

LOS 49.a Explain
CFAI p. 188, Schweser p. 270

Introduction to Industry and Company Analysis

Uses of Industry Analysis

Understanding a firm's business environment—growth, competition, risks

Active management—industry analysis can be used to weight a portfolio and rotate among industries

Performance attribution—industry selection as a source of portfolio return

© Kaplan, Inc.   17

LOS 49.b Compare/Classify
CFAI p. 189, Schweser p. 270

Introduction to Industry and Company Analysis

Approaches to Industry Groupings

1. **Products and services**: Group by sector, industry, or primary business activity (e.g., health care, insurance, software, beer)

   There are various commercial and government industry classification systems

2. **Business cycle sensitivity**

3. **Statistical groupings**: Group firms with high historical returns correlations

© Kaplan, Inc.   18

LOS 49.c Explain
CFAI p. 190, Schweser p. 273

Introduction to Industry and Company Analysis

Business Cycle Sensitivity

Cyclical: Earnings *highly dependent* on the business cycle (e.g., energy, financials, industrials, materials, commodities, consumer discretionary, technology)

Non-cyclical: Earnings *less dependent* on business cycle

   Defensive: Basic goods and services with relatively stable demand (e.g., consumer staples, utilities, health care, telecommunications)

   Growth: Demand is so strong the firm is largely unaffected by business cycles

© Kaplan, Inc.   19

Peer Groups

Start with narrowest industry classification:

1. Find specific competitors—annual report

2. Find comparable companies—industry reports, management comments

3. Determine similar business model/activity

Peer group companies should have similar:

- Business activities
- Demand drivers
- Cost structure drivers
- Availability of capital

Elements of Industry Analysis

- Classify industries within **life-cycle stage**

- Position industry on **experience curve** (cost per unit relative to output)

- Consider demographic, macroeconomic, governmental, social, and technological influences

- Examine **forces that determine industry competition** → → →

Porter's Five Forces

Intensity of industry competition depends on:

1. Rivalry among existing competitors
2. Threat of entry
3. Threat of substitutes
4. Power of buyers
5. Power of suppliers

Strategies:
Cost leadership or differentiated products

Barriers to Entry

High barriers to entry (low potential competition):

- Industry may have low rivalry among existing firms
- Firms tend to have greater pricing power as a result

Low barriers to entry (competitors can easily enter):

- Industry competition likely intense
- Firms tend to have low pricing power

Barriers to entry and competitive environment may change over time

Industry Concentration

High industry concentration:
Often indicates low competitive rivalry and that firms have pricing power (not always)

Low industry concentration (fragmented market):
Strong indicator of highly competitive industry and little pricing power

© Kaplan, Inc.

24

Industry Capacity

Undercapacity (demand exceeds supply):
Low competitive rivalry and high pricing power

Overcapacity:
Leads to strong price competition and little pricing power, especially when barriers to exit are high

- Analysts should also consider how capacity conditions can be expected to change over time
  - Physical capacity comes into production more slowly than non-physical capacity

© Kaplan, Inc.

25

Market Share Stability

Highly variable market shares:
Suggest highly competitive industry and little pricing power for existing firms

Stable market shares suggest less intense competition and more pricing power

High **switching costs** contribute to market share stability

© Kaplan, Inc.

26

Industry Life Cycle

Embryonic stage: Slow growth, high prices, large investment required, high risk of failure

Growth stage: Rapid demand growth, low competition, falling prices, increasing profitability

Shakeout stage: Slower growth, intense competition, increasing overcapacity, declining profitability, cost cutting, increased failures

© Kaplan, Inc.

27

Industry Life Cycle

Mature stage: Slow growth, industry consolidation, high barriers to entry including brand loyalty and efficient cost structure

- Superior products lead to market share increases

- With stable demand, firms avoid price competition

- During economic downturns, overcapacity can lead to intense price competition

© Kaplan, Inc.

28

Industry Life Cycle

Decline stage: Negative growth, excess capacity leads to price competition, higher production costs as demand falls, weak companies merge or exit

Reasons for decline:

- Technology: Decline of newspapers

- Global competition: Decline of U.S. textile industry

- Social change and changing tastes: Declining beer sales per capita in Germany

© Kaplan, Inc.

29

Limitations of Life-Cycle Analysis

- Most useful during stable periods

- Stages may not be as long as anticipated or might be skipped altogether

- Some firms will experience dissimilar growth and profits due to competitive position

© Kaplan, Inc.

30

Which of the following is *most likely* descriptive of the industry stage characterized by high prices and slow growth?

A. Mature.

B. Decline.

C. Embryonic.

© Kaplan, Inc.

31 - 1

Which factor is *most likely* associated with stable market share?

A. Low switching costs.

B. Low barriers to entry.

C. Slow pace of product innovation.

33 - 1

Equity Analysis and Valuation

50. Equity Valuation: Concepts and Basic Tools

KAPLAN UNIVERSITY   SCHOOL OF PROFESSIONAL AND CONTINUING EDUCATION   SCHWESER

External Industry Influences on Growth, Profitability, and Risk

Macroeconomic factors: Economic growth, interest rates, credit availability, inflation

Technology: New or improved products

Demographics: Age distribution, population

Social influences: How people conduct their lives and choose to spend their incomes

Government: Tax rates, business regulation, purchases

© Kaplan, Inc.

32

Additional Learning Outcomes

LOS 49.i: characteristics of representative industries (see CFA Curriculum Vol. 5, pp. 219–221, Exhibit 7)

LOS 49.k: elements of company analysis (see CFA Curriculum Vol. 5, pp. 229–232, Exhibit 8)

© Kaplan, Inc.

34

Equity Valuation: Concepts
and Basic Tools

Types of Equity Valuation Models

1. **Discounted Cash Flow Models**

2. **Multiplier Models**

3. **Asset-Based Valuation**

© Kaplan, Inc.

37

Equity Valuation: Concepts
and Basic Tools

Dividend Discount Model

$$V_0 = \sum_{t=1}^{\infty} \frac{D_t}{(1+k_e)^t}$$

- Corporation has an indefinite life
- Investor must receive future cash dividends to be willing to invest today

© Kaplan, Inc.

39

Equity Valuation: Concepts
and Basic Tools

Security Valuation

Market price < estimated value: **undervalued**

Market price > estimated value: **overvalued**

- For security valuation to be profitable, the security must be misvalued now and must <u>converge towards intrinsic value in the future</u>

- Market price is more likely to be "correct" when a security is followed by many analysts

© Kaplan, Inc.

36

Equity Valuation: Concepts
and Basic Tools

Valuing Common Stock

A stock paid a $1.50 dividend last year that will grow at 8% every year. You require a 12% return and you expect the stock price to be $51.00 at the end of Year 3. What is the stock's value today?

$$\frac{1.50(1.08)}{1.12} + \frac{1.50(1.08)^2}{1.12^2} + \frac{1.50(1.08)^3}{1.12^3} + \frac{51.00}{1.12^3} = \$40.50$$

© Kaplan, Inc.

38 – 4

LOS 50.d Calculate
CFAI p. 251, Schweser p. 295

Preferred Stock Valuation

Preferred stock (usually) has no maturity date and pays a fixed dividend

$$V_0 = \frac{\text{Preferred dividend}}{k_P}$$

A $100 par value 7% preferred pays an annual dividend of $7.

If the required rate of return is 8%, it will trade at 7 / 0.08 = $87.50.

© Kaplan, Inc.

41

LOS 50.e Calculate/Interpret
CFAI p. 254, Schweser p. 296

Constant Growth Model

A stock paid a dividend of $1.50 per share last year, which is expected to grow at a rate of 8.0% forever. If an investor requires a 12% return, what is the value of the stock today?

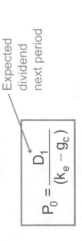

This is D_0

$$= \frac{1.50 \ (1+0.08)}{(0.12 - 0.08)} = \$40.50$$

© Kaplan, Inc.

43 - 1

LOS 50.c Explain/Describe
CFAI p. 248, Schweser p. 292

Free Cash Flow to Equity Model

$$V_0 = \sum_{t=1}^{\infty} \frac{FCFE_t}{(1+k_e)^t}$$

FCFE: Cash available after a firm meets its debt obligations and necessary capital expenditures

FCFE = CFO − FCInv + Net borrowing

© Kaplan, Inc.

40

LOS 50.e Calculate/Interpret
CFAI p. 254, Schweser p. 296

Gordon (Constant) Growth Model

- Dividends grow at a constant rate forever
- k_e must be greater than g_c

Expected dividend next period

$$P_0 = \frac{D_1}{(k_e - g_c)}$$

where g_c = constant dividend growth rate

© Kaplan, Inc.

42

LOS 50.e Calculate/Interpret
CFAI p. 254, Schweser p. 296

Estimating the Value of *g*

***g* represents the earnings and dividend growth rate in the constant growth model**

g = (RR)(ROE)

where:

RR = earnings retention rate = (1 – payout ratio)

ROE = return on equity

© Kaplan, Inc.

44

LOS 50.e Calculate/Interpret
CFAI p. 254, Schweser p. 296

Acme has an ROE of 18%, EPS of $2.00 for last year, and paid a dividend of $1.20. If the ROE and payout ratio remain the same and the required rate of return is 13%, the value of the stock according to the constant growth model is *closest* to:

A. $22.18.

B. $40.24.

C. $60.44.

© Kaplan, Inc.

45 - 2

LOS 50.e Calculate/Interpret
CFAI p. 254, Schweser p. 296

Multistage DDM

- For companies experiencing temporary rapid growth

- Assumes that dividend growth will be constant at some future date

- Estimate dividends during the rapid growth period

- Use Gordon growth model to find the terminal value of the firm when growth is constant

© Kaplan, Inc.

46

LOS 50.e Calculate/Interpret
CFAI p. 254, Schweser p. 296

Multistage DDM Example

Calculate the value of a stock given:

- Last year's dividend = $1.00

- Dividend will grow at 15% for two years

- Dividend will grow at 5% after two years

- Required return is 11%

© Kaplan, Inc.

47

Multistage DDM Example

Step 1: Forecast the dividend for each year of rapid growth and for the first year of constant growth

$D_1 = \$1.00(1.15)^1 = \$1.15$

$D_2 = \$1.00(1.15)^2 = \$1.32$

$D_3 = \$1.00(1.15)^2 (1.05) = \$1.39$

Identify the first dividend that will grow at a constant growth rate

© Kaplan, Inc.

48

Multistage DDM Example

Step 2: Use the constant growth model to find the value of the stock one period before the dividend that will grow at a constant rate (D_2)

Using: $P_1 = D_2 / (k - g)$

We have: $\$1.32 / (0.11 - 0.05) = \$22.00$

© Kaplan, Inc.

49

Multistage DDM Example

Step 3: Find the PV of expected dividends and of the expected future stock price

$P_0 = \dfrac{D_1}{1+k} + \dfrac{P_1}{1+k}$, where $P_1 = \dfrac{D_2}{k-g}$

$P_0 = \dfrac{1.15}{1.11} + \dfrac{22.00}{1.11} = \$20.86$

$22.00 = \dfrac{1.32}{0.11-0.05}$

© Kaplan, Inc.

50

A stock is not expected to pay dividends until three years from now. The dividend is then expected to be $2.00 per share. If the required rate of return is 12%, and the dividend is expected to grow at 9% the value of the stock today is *closest* to:

A. $41.
B. $53.
C. $67.

© Kaplan, Inc.

51-2

LOS 50.f Identify
CFAI p. 257, Schweser p. 301   Equity Valuation: Concepts
and Basic Tools

Dividend Discount Model Use

Gordon growth model is most appropriate for firms that pay a dividend that will grow at a constant rate, such as:

- Stable and mature firms
- Noncyclical firms

© Kaplan, Inc.   52

LOS 50.f Identify
CFAI p. 257, Schweser p. 301   Equity Valuation: Concepts
and Basic Tools

Dividend Discount Model Use

2-stage DDM appropriate for:

- Firms with high current growth that will fall to a stable rate in the future
- Older firms that were in the constant growth phase, but are now in a high growth phase or are losing market share

3-stage DDM appropriate for:

- Young firms still in the high growth phase

© Kaplan, Inc.   53

LOS 50.g Explain/Distinguish
CFAI p. 263, Schweser p. 302   Equity Valuation: Concepts
and Basic Tools

P/E Based on Fundamentals

Begin with the constant growth value:

$$P_0 = \frac{D_1}{k - g}$$

Divide both sides of the equation by next year's projected earnings (E_1) to get P/E:

$$\frac{P_0}{E_1} = \frac{D_1/E_1}{k - g}$$

$\frac{D_1}{E_1}$ — Dividend Payout Ratio

$\frac{P_0}{E_1}$ = (leading) price to earnings ratio

© Kaplan, Inc.   54

LOS 50.g Explain/Distinguish
CFAI p. 263, Schweser p. 302   Equity Valuation: Concepts
and Basic Tools

P/E Based on Fundamentals

$$\frac{P_0}{E_1} = \frac{D_1/E_1}{k - g}$$

Other things equal, fundamental P/E ratio (price) is higher if firm has:

- Higher dividend payout ratio
- Higher growth rate
- Lower required return

Note that increasing the payout ratio will decrease the growth rate: g = ROE × (1 − payout ratio)

© Kaplan, Inc.   55

Slide 56-3 (P/E Based on Fundamentals)

P/E Based on Fundamentals

You expect a firm to pay out 30% of its earnings as dividends. Earnings and dividends are expected to grow at a constant rate of 6%. If you require a 13% return on the stock, what is the stock's expected P/E ratio?

$$\frac{P_0}{E_1} = \frac{D_1 / E_1}{k - g} = \frac{0.30}{0.13 - 0.06} = 4.3 \times$$

© Kaplan, Inc.

56 - 3

Slide 57 (Price Multiples)

Price Multiples

P/E = stock price / earnings per share

P/S = stock price / sales per share

P/B = stock price / book value per share,
(sometimes market-to-book)

P/CF = stock price / cash flow per share, where cash flow = operating cash flow or free cash flow

© Kaplan, Inc.

57

Slide 58 (Using Price Multiple Comparables)

Using Price Multiple Comparables

Based on the **law of one price**: Two comparable assets should sell for the same multiple

P/E, P/S, P/B, or P/CF ratio lower than industry average or comparable stock suggests stock is undervalued

This is an example of **relative valuation**

© Kaplan, Inc.

58

Slide 59 (Enterprise Value Multiple)

Enterprise Value Multiple

Enterprise Value (EV)
$$\frac{\text{Enterprise Value (EV)}}{\text{EBITDA}}$$

EV = Market value of common stock
+ market value of debt
− cash and short-term investments

Useful when:
- Firms have different capital structures
- Earnings are negative, can't use P/E ratio

© Kaplan, Inc.

59

Slide 60

EV / EBITDA Multiple Example

Stock price	$40.00
Shares outstanding	200,000
Market value of long-term debt	$600,000
BV of long-term debt	$900,000
BV of total debt and liabilities	$2,100,000
Cash and marketable securities	$250,000
EBITDA	$1,000,000

© Kaplan, Inc.

60

Slide 61

EV / EBITDA Multiple Example

Step 1: Determine market value of short-term debt and liabilities

Assume book value = market value for short-term items

Market value of short-term debt estimated as:

BV of total debt – BV of long-term debt =

$2,100,000 – $900,000 = $1,200,000

© Kaplan, Inc.

61

Slide 62

EV / EBITDA Multiple Example

Step 2: Market value of total debt = market value of long-term debt + short-term debt

= $600,000 + $1,200,000 = $1,800,000

Step 3: Market value of equity = stock price × number of shares

= $40 × 200,000 = $8,000,000

© Kaplan, Inc.

62

Slide 63

EV / EBITDA Multiple Example

Step 4: EV = debt + equity – cash

= $1,800,000 + $8,000,000 – $250,000

= $9,550,000

Step 5: EV / EBITDA

= $9,550,000 / $1,000,000 = 9.6×

Step 6: Compare to competitor or industry average, low values indicate underpriced

© Kaplan, Inc.

63

LOS 50.j Describe
CFAI p. 274, Schweser p. 308

Asset-Based Models

Equity equals market or fair value of assets minus liabilities

Analysts usually adjust asset book values to market values

Asset-based valuation models provide a floor value, estimate of value in liquidation

© Kaplan, Inc.

64

LOS 50.k Explain
CFAI p. 246, Schweser p. 310

Present Value Models

Advantages:

- Theoretically sound
- Widely accepted

Disadvantages:

- Inputs must be estimated
- Valuation can be very sensitive to input values

© Kaplan, Inc.

65

LOS 50.k Explain
CFAI p. 246, Schweser p. 310

Multiplier Models

Advantages:

- Widely used, associated with stock returns
- Easily calculated and readily available
- Good for identifying attractive companies in an industry
- Useful for time-series or cross-sectional analysis

Disadvantages:

- Differences in accounting methods reduce comparability
- Multiples for cyclical companies highly variable

© Kaplan, Inc.

66

LOS 50.k Explain
CFAI p. 246, Schweser p. 310

Asset-Based Models

Advantages:

- Can provide floor values
- Useful for firm with mostly tangible short-term assets or if firm is to be liquidated

Disadvantages:

- Ongoing firm value may be greater than asset value, does not reflect future cash flows
- Fair values of assets can be difficult to estimate; especially with primarily intangible assets, high inflation environments

© Kaplan, Inc.

67

Additional Problems

Additional Problems

2) Free cash flow to equity would be best measured as:

A. CFO minus fixed capital investment minus net borrowing.

B. total cash flow plus financing cash flow minus investing cash flow.

C. CFO minus debt principal payments plus debt issued minus fixed capital investment.

- 1

LOS 50.k Explain

CFAI p. 246, Schweser p. 310

Equity Valuation: Concepts and Basic Tools

Choice of Valuation Model

- Model should be chosen based on available inputs

- Model should be chosen based on the intended use of the valuation

- More complexity is not necessarily better

- Consider values using more than one method

- Consider uncertainty about input values

- Consider uncertainty about the appropriateness of the model

68

CFA Curriculum Vol. 5,

R.50, Q.36, p. 285

1) Which of the following is *most likely* considered a weakness of present value models?

A. Present value models cannot be used for companies that do not pay dividends.

B. Small changes in model assumptions and inputs can result in large changes in the computed intrinsic value of the security.

C. The value of the security depends on the investor's holding period; thus, comparing valuations of different companies for different investors is difficult.

- 1

CFA Curriculum Vol. 5,
R.50, Q.28, p. 284

3) The market value of equity for a company can be calculated as enterprise value:

A. minus market value of debt, preferred stock, and short-term investments.

B. plus market value of debt and preferred stock minus short-term investments.

C. minus market value of debt and preferred stock plus short-term investments.

- 5

STUDY SESSION 14 ANSWERS

Reading	Slide Number	Answer
48	12	A
48	14	A
49	31	C
49	33	C
50	45	A
50	51	B

Additional Problems

1. B

2. C

3. C

Study Session 15

Fixed Income: Basic Concepts

Fixed Income

Fixed Income: Basic Concepts

51. Fixed-Income Securities: Defining Elements

KAPLAN UNIVERSITY SCHOOL OF PROFESSIONAL AND CONTINUING EDUCATION | SCHWESER

Fixed Income

Study Session 15
Fixed Income: Basic Concepts

51. Fixed-Income Securities: Defining Elements
52. Fixed-Income Markets: Issuance, Trading, and Funding
53. Introduction to Fixed-Income Valuation
54. Introduction to Asset-Backed Securities

KAPLAN UNIVERSITY SCHOOL OF PROFESSIONAL AND CONTINUING EDUCATION | SCHWESER

© Kaplan, Inc.

Fixed-Income Securities: Defining Elements

LOS 51.b,c Describe/Compare/Identify
CFAI p. 303, Schweser p. 3

Bond Indenture

- **Trust deed or indenture:** Legal contract between issuer and bondholder, held by trustee

- **Covenants:** Provisions of an indenture

- **Affirmative covenants:** Actions the issuer must perform (e.g., make payments on time, insure assets, comply with laws)

- **Negative covenants:** Restrictions on issuer actions that would disadvantage bondholders (e.g., cannot pay dividends until bond payments made)

© Kaplan, Inc.

3

Fixed-Income Securities: Defining Elements

LOS 51.a Describe
CFAI p. 297, Schweser p. 1

Basic Features

- **Issuer:** Entity that pays interest, repays principal

- **Maturity date:** Date of final payment

- **Tenor:** Time to maturity at any point in time

- **Par (face) value:** Principal to be repaid

- **Coupon rate:** Annual interest as percent of par

- **Coupon frequency:** Number of payments per year, also periodicity

- **Currency** denomination (e.g., euros, pounds, yen)

© Kaplan, Inc.

2

Domestic and Foreign Bonds

Domestic bonds: Domestic issuer and currency ($US Microsoft bonds, issued in the United States)

Foreign bonds: Foreign issuer, trade in domestic currency ($US Heineken bonds issued in the United States)

National bond market: Includes trading of both types of issues

© Kaplan, Inc.

4

Eurobonds

- Sold by an international syndicate, issued simultaneously to investors in many countries

- Issued outside the jurisdiction of any single country, often *bearer* bonds rather than *registered* bonds

- Issued in a currency other than the issuer's domestic currency (e.g., euroyen, eurodollar bonds)

© Kaplan, Inc.

5

Eurobonds

Advantages of eurobonds:

- Avoid regulation, less tax constraints, issue USD bonds without registering with the SEC (cannot be traded in the United States)

- Reach a large pool of investors globally, primarily in the eurozone, Asia-Pacific, and the United States

Global bonds: Eurobonds that also trade in a domestic bond market (e.g., World Bank bonds)

© Kaplan, Inc.

6

Collateral

Unsecured bonds: Claim to issuer's overall assets and cash flows

Secured bonds: Claim to specific asset owned by issuer (asset is pledged as <u>collateral</u>)

Collateral trust bonds: Securities held by trustee

Equipment trust certificates: Physical assets owned by trust, leased to firm

Secured bonds have <u>seniority</u> over unsecured bonds

© Kaplan, Inc.

7

Covered Bonds

Legislation protects assets segregated, but still owned by the firm and on the firm's balance sheet

- Primarily issued by financial firms

- Firm must augment assets whenever they are insufficient to support the covered bonds

- Bondholders effectively have recourse to the firm as well as the segregated financial assets

© Kaplan, Inc.

8

Credit Enhancement

External

Bank guarantee – issued by bank

Surety bond – insurance company

Letter of credit – financial institution

⎱ Provided by third party
⎰ Counterparty risk

Cash collateral account: Cash borrowed by issuer, invested in low-risk short-term debt securities at inception

© Kaplan, Inc.

9

Credit Enhancement

Internal: Built into structure of bond issue

Overcollateralization: Collateral value is greater than amount borrowed

Excess spread: Yield on asset pool is greater than yield of bonds issued

Tranches: Different priority of claims for different bond classes, waterfall structure

© Kaplan, Inc.

10

Tax Considerations

Original issue discount (OID) bonds

- Bonds issued with coupon < market rate

- Price increase from passage of time is typically taxed as <u>interest</u> income annually

Zero-coupon (pure discount) bonds

- Pay only par value at maturity

- May require annual payments for taxes

© Kaplan, Inc.

11

LOS 51.e Describe
CFAI p. 316, Schweser p. 7

Fixed-Income Securities:
Defining Elements

Fixed Income Cash Flows

Bullet structure: Interest only on coupon dates, all principal repaid at maturity (plain-vanilla bond)

Partially amortizing: Periodic payments include interest and principal, with balloon payment of remaining principal at maturity

Fully amortizing: Equal payments each period include interest and principal (e.g., mortgage loan)

Sinking fund: Some bonds are retired or redeemed early on scheduled dates

© Kaplan, Inc.

12

LOS 51.e Describe
CFAI p. 316, Schweser p. 7

Fixed-Income Securities:
Defining Elements

Fixed Income Cash Flows

Floating-rate notes (FRN): Coupon rate based on a reference rate (e.g., 6-month Libor) plus or minus a fixed margin (e.g., +80 bp) for issue risk. May have:

- **Cap**, maximum rate regardless of reference rate and margin (benefits <u>issuer</u>)

- **Floor**, minimum rate regardless of reference rate and margin (benefits <u>bondholder</u>)

Variable-rate note: Margin not fixed

Inverse floater: Coupon rate = X% − reference rate

© Kaplan, Inc.

13

LOS 51.e Describe
CFAI p. 316, Schweser p. 7

Fixed-Income Securities:
Defining Elements

Fixed Income Cash Flows

Index-linked Bonds

Coupon rate or principal changes based on value of a published index

- <u>Inflation-indexed bonds (CPI)</u>

- <u>Equity-linked notes (equity index)</u>

- <u>Commodity-indexed bonds</u>
  [commodity price, e.g., gold, oil]

© Kaplan, Inc.

14

LOS 51.e Describe
CFAI p. 316, Schweser p. 7

Fixed-Income Securities:
Defining Elements

Fixed Income Cash Flows

Inflation-linked bonds (linkers) have payments that are adjusted based on CPI

Interest-indexed: Coupon rate adjusted

Capital-indexed: Principal (par) value adjusted, coupon rate remains fixed (e.g., TIPS, zeros)

Indexed-annuity bonds: Fully amortizing, payments adjusted

Principal-protected: Pay original face value if index decreases over life of bond

© Kaplan, Inc.

15

Embedded Options

Contingency provisions (embedded options) are actions the issuer or bondholder may take

Callable bonds: Issuer may redeem bonds before maturity on scheduled call date(s) at specified call price(s)

- Bonds may have a period of call protection
- Make-whole provision: Call price includes present value of future coupons

© Kaplan, Inc.

17

All else equal, which of the following types of bonds will offer the greatest YTM at issuance?

A. Putable bond.

B. Callable bond.

C. Convertible bond.

© Kaplan, Inc.

19 - 1

A 3-year bond has a coupon rate of 100 basis points above 180-day LIBOR and pays its par value at maturity. This bond:

A. is index-linked.

B. has a bullet structure.

C. is a variable-rate note.

© Kaplan, Inc.

16 - 2

Embedded Options

Putable bonds: Bondholder may sell bond back to issuer, typically for par value

Convertible bonds: Bondholder may exchange bond for issuer's common stock

Warrants: Right to buy issuer's common shares at a given price (attached to straight bond; bondholder does not exchange bond)

Contingent convertibles: Convert to common stock automatically if specified event occurs

© Kaplan, Inc.

18

Fixed Income

Fixed Income: Basic Concepts

52. Fixed-Income Markets: Issuance, Trading, and Funding

KAPLAN UNIVERSITY SCHOOL OF PROFESSIONAL AND CONTINUING EDUCATION | SCHWESER

Interbank Money Market

Interest rates for unsecured lending between banks

Libor: London interbank offered rate

Libor quoted for 10 currencies,

15 maturities from overnight to 12 months

150 rates quoted, all as annualized rates

Quoted as annualized rates using 360/days

Other sources:

Euribor: European interbank offered rate

Tibor, Sibor, Hibor, Koribor,...

© Kaplan, Inc.

21

Primary Market for Bonds

Public offering: Register issue with securities regulators

Private placement: Sold only to qualified investors, not offered to public

Shelf registration: Register entire issue with regulators, issue bonds over time

© Kaplan, Inc.

22

Primary Market for Bonds

Underwritten offerings

Investment bank or bank syndicate buys entire issue, resells to dealers and investors

Bonds sometimes trade for forward delivery in the "when-issued" or "grey" market

Best-efforts offerings

Investment banks sell bonds on commission basis

Auctions

Often used for government bonds (primary dealers)

© Kaplan, Inc.

23

LOS 52.d Describe
CFAI p. 363, Schweser p. 22

Secondary Market for Bonds

Primarily over-the-counter trading (dealer markets)

Bid-ask spread depends on issue's liquidity

Trade settlement

✓ Typically T + 2 or T + 3 for corporate bonds

✓ T + 1 for government, quasi-government bonds

✓ Same day (cash settlement) for many money market securities and some government bonds

© Kaplan, Inc.

24

LOS 52.e,f Describe
CFAI p. 365, Schweser p. 22

Government Debt

Sovereign bonds: Issued by national governments

■ Issued in local currency or foreign currency

■ Higher credit rating for local currency debt than for developed country currency debt

Nonsovereign government bonds

■ States, provinces, counties, cities

■ May be paid from taxes, fees, or revenues from specific projects

© Kaplan, Inc.

25

LOS 52.f Describe
CFAI p. 369, Schweser p. 23

Agency Debt

Quasi-government bonds or agency bonds: Issued by government-sponsored entities

■ Example: Fannie Mae (U.S.)

■ May be guaranteed by national government

Supranational bonds: Issued by multilateral agencies

■ Examples: IMF, World Bank

© Kaplan, Inc.

26

LOS 52.g Describe
CFAI p. 371, Schweser p. 23

Corporate Debt

Bank borrowing

Bilateral loan: Single bank

Syndicated loan: Multiple banks

Commercial paper (working capital, bridge financing)

U.S. commercial paper: Maturities up to 270 days, sold on a *discount interest* basis, settles T + 0

Eurocommercial paper: Maturities up to 364 days, may be sold on *discount interest* or *add-on interest* basis, settles T + 2

© Kaplan, Inc.

27

Corporate Debt

Commercial paper (cont.)

Rollover risk: The risk that new paper cannot be issued to pay for maturing paper

- Deterioration of credit
- Systemic failure

✓ Firms have backup lines of credit to get acceptable credit ratings

✓ Funds available unless there is a *material adverse change*

© Kaplan, Inc.

28

Add-on vs. Discount Yield

Consider 240-day commercial paper with holding period yield of 1.35%

Discount yield: Priced at 100 / 1.0135 = 98.668

Pay 100 at maturity

Discount from par = 100 − 98.668 = 1.332%

Add-on yield: Priced at 100

Pay 100(1.0135) = 101.35 at maturity

© Kaplan, Inc.

29

Corporate Debt

Corporate bonds

Term maturity structure: Entire issue matures on same date

Serial bond issue: Multiple maturity dates

Medium-term Notes (MTNs)

Issuer provides range of maturities, buyer specifies desired value and maturity

Continuous offering by issuer's agent

© Kaplan, Inc.

30

Repurchase Agreements

- Source of short-term funding for bond dealers

- Sell bond to counterparty and agree to repurchase it on **repo date** at a slightly higher price

- 1 day = **overnight repo**, > 1 day = **term repo**

Repo rate is percent difference between sale price and repurchase price.

© Kaplan, Inc.

31

LOS 52.i Describe
CFAI p. 384, Schweser p. 26

Repurchase Agreements

Repo rate (interest) and repo margin (haircut):

Decrease with higher credit quality of collateral and when security is in greater demand

 lower return, less protection

Increase with the term of the repo (maturity)

 higher return, more protection

Repo rate is lower when delivery is required
Repo margin is lower when counterparty credit is better

© Kaplan, Inc.

33

LOS 52.i Describe
CFAI p. 384, Schweser p. 26

Risks of Repurchase Agreements

Both parties in a repo agreement face **counterparty risk**

Lender of funds (buyer of security) has the risk that the value of the security is less than the repo price, and the borrower (seller) does not repurchase the security on the repo date

This risk can be reduced by lending less than the market value of the collateral security

Repo margin (haircut) is percentage difference between sale price and value of bond

© Kaplan, Inc.

32

Fixed Income:
Basic Concepts

53. Introduction to
Fixed-Income Valuation

KAPLAN SCHOOL OF PROFESSIONAL
UNIVERSITY AND CONTINUING EDUCATION | **SCHWESER**

Additional Learning Outcomes

LOS 52.a: classifications of fixed income markets

LOS 52.h: short-term funding for banks

© Kaplan, Inc.

34

8% Annual-Pay Bond Cash Flows Per $100 of Par Value

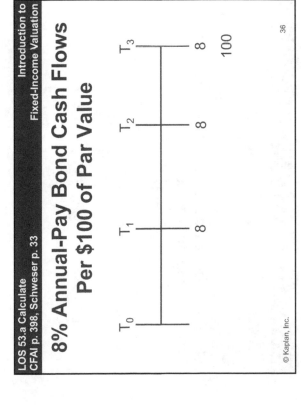

36

Calculating a Bond's Price

3-year, 8% annual coupon, market discount rate (required rate of return or required yield) = 12%.

$$\frac{8}{(1.12)} + \frac{8}{(1.12)^2} + \frac{8+100}{(1.12)^3} = 90.393$$

N = 3; PMT = 8; FV = 100; I/Y = 12; **PV = −90.393**

37 - 1

Calculating a Market Discount Rate

3-year, 8% annual coupon bond, priced at 90.393

Calculate the market discount rate (IRR).

N = 3; PMT = 8; FV = 100; PV = −90.393 ; I/Y = **12%**

This is the **yield-to-maturity (YTM)** and assumes:

1. Held-to-maturity
2. All payments made
3. Coupon payments reinvested at YTM

38

Calculate the price of a $1,000 3-year 8% semiannual-pay bond with a YTM of 12%.

39 - 6

LOS 53.b Identify
CFAI p. 403, Schweser p. 35

Relationships

Yield up → Price down; Price down → Yield up
Yield down → Price up; Price up → Yield down

coupon rate > YTM → price > par (premium)

coupon < YTM → price < par (discount)

© Kaplan, Inc.

41

LOS 53.b Identify
CFAI p. 403, Schweser p. 35

Price-Yield Relationship
Semiannual-Pay 8% 3-year Bond

At 4%:   I/Y = 2%   N = 6   FV = 1,000   PMT = 40
            CPT PV = $1,112.03

At 8%:   I/Y = 4%   N = 6   FV = 1,000   PMT = 40
            CPT PV = $1,000.00

At 12%:   I/Y = 6%   N = 6   FV = 1,000   PMT = 40
            CPT PV = $901.65

© Kaplan, Inc.

43 - 3

A zero-coupon bond matures in 3 years. At a YTM
on a semi-annual basis of 8%, the value per 100 of
face value is:

A. 79.031.

B. 79.383.

C. 79.574.

© Kaplan, Inc.

40 - 3

LOS 53.b Identify
CFAI p. 403, Schweser p. 35

Relationships

Convexity

Price increase from decrease in yield is larger than
price decrease from increase in yield.

Maturity Effect

Other things equal, values of bonds with longer
maturities are more sensitive to changes in YTM.

Coupon Effect

Other things equal, values of bonds with lower
coupons are more sensitive to changes in YTM.

© Kaplan, Inc.

42

LOS 53.b Identify
CFAI p. 403, Schweser p. 35

Constant-Yield Price Trajectory

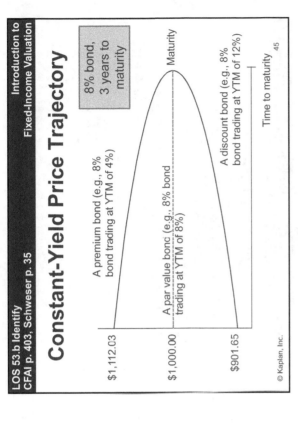

8% bond,
3 years to
maturity

A premium bond (e.g., 8%
bond trading at YTM of 4%)

Maturity

$1,112.03

A par value bond (e.g., 8% bond
trading at YTM of 8%)

$1,000.00

A discount bond (e.g., 8%
bond trading at YTM of 12%)

$901.65

Time to maturity

© Kaplan, Inc.   45

LOS 53.c Define/Calculate
CFAI p. 407, Schweser p. 37

Spot Rates

A **spot rate** is a market discount rate for a <u>single</u>
<u>payment</u> to be received in the future.

Yields on zero-coupon bonds are spot rates, also
called zero rates, denoted Z_1, Z_2, Z_3.

© Kaplan, Inc.   47

LOS 53.b Identify
CFAI p. 403, Schweser p. 35

Option-Free Bond Price-Yield
Curve

Price

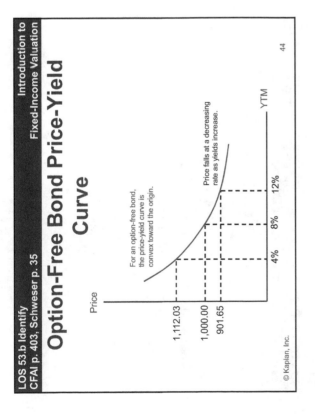

For an option-free bond,
the price-yield curve is
convex toward the origin.

Price falls at a decreasing
rate as yields increase.

1,112.03

1,000.00
901.65

4%   8%   12%

YTM

© Kaplan, Inc.   44

A 6%, 10-year semiannual coupon bond has a YTM
of 8%:

1. What is the price of the bond per 100 par value?

2. What is the value after 1 year if the yield does not
   change?

3. What is the value after 2 years if the yield does
   not change?

© Kaplan, Inc.   46 – 3

Bond Valuation With Spot Rates

Value a 3-year, $1,000, 3% annual coupon bond:

Spot rates: $Z_1 = 2.5\%$, $Z_2 = 3.0\%$, $Z_3 = 3.5\%$

Maturity	Annual rate	Cash flow	PV of cash flow
1 year	2.5%	$30	$29.27
2 years	3.0%	$30	$28.28
3 years	3.5%	$1,030	$929.00

$986.55

© Kaplan, Inc.

48

Bond Values Using Spot Rates

Value a 3-year 3% annual coupon bond:

$Z_1 = 2.5\%$, $Z_2 = 3\%$, $Z_3 = 3.5\%$

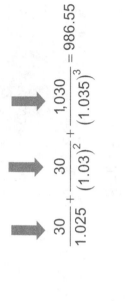

$$\frac{30}{1.025} + \frac{30}{(1.03)^2} + \frac{1,030}{(1.035)^3} = 986.55$$

© Kaplan, Inc.

49

Spot Rates and YTM

Using spot rates, we valued the $1,000 3-year 3% annual coupon bond at $986.55

We can use this value to calculate the YTM

$N = 3$, $PV = -986.55$, $PMT = 30$, $FV = 1,000$, CPT I/Y = 3.48%

$$\frac{30}{1.0348} + \frac{30}{(1.0348)^2} + \frac{1,030}{(1.0348)^3} = 986.55$$

© Kaplan, Inc.

50

Accrued Interest

Investor buys a $1,000 par value bond with a 4% annual coupon paid on May 15. The trade settles on August 10.

Accrued interest - 30/360 (corporates):

15 (May) + 30 (June) + 30 (July) + 10 (August) = 85 days; 85/360 × $40 = $9.44

Accrued interest - actual/actual (governments):

16 (May) + 30 (June) + 31 (July) + 10 (August) = 87 days; 87/365 × $40 = $9.53

© Kaplan, Inc.

51

Flat and Full Prices

Full price (invoice price or dirty price)

= Price including accrued interest at settlement

Flat price (clean price or quoted price)

= Full price − accrued interest.

© Kaplan, Inc.

52

Flat and Full Prices

Annual coupon rate = 6%	YTM = 7%
Frequency = semiannual	Feb. 15 and Aug. 15
Face value = $100,000	Maturity: Aug 15, 2035

What is the full price based on 30/360 method if the bond is purchased to settle on Nov. 20, 2015?

Value on Aug 15, 2015 = 89.32

Days since coupon = 15 + 30 + 30 + 20 = 95

$$\text{Full price} = 89.32246 \,(1.035)^{95/180} = 90.95904 \times 1{,}000 = 90{,}959.04$$

$$\text{Accrued interest} = 3{,}000 \times \frac{95}{180} = 1{,}583.33$$

$$\text{Flat price} = 90{,}959.04 - 1{,}583.33 = 89{,}375.71$$

© Kaplan, Inc.

53 - 5

Matrix Pricing

Use matrix pricing when bonds trade infrequently so that market YTM is unavailable.

Matrix pricing uses YTMs of traded bonds of <u>same credit quality</u> to estimate bond YTM.

1. Use average of YTMs for same maturity

2. Use linear interpolation to adjust for differences in maturities

© Kaplan, Inc.

54

Matrix Pricing

Estimate YTM for a nontraded 3-year, annual-pay bond rated A+ based on the following bonds rated A+:

2-year, YTM 4.3%

5-year, YTM 5.1% ⎤
                    ⎬ Average 5-year YTM = 5.2%
5-year, YTM 5.3% ⎦

Interpolate 3-year YTM:

$$4.3\% + [(3 - 2)/(5 - 2)](5.2 - 4.3) = \mathbf{4.6\%}$$

4.3   4.6   4.9   5.2

© Kaplan, Inc.

55 - 3

An annual-pay bond has a YTM of 14%.

The yield for this bond stated on a semiannual-bond basis is:

A. 13.54%.

B. 13.86%.

C. 14.49%.

Current Yield

Current yield = $\dfrac{\text{annual coupon payment}}{\text{flat price}}$

For an 8%, 3-year (semiannual-pay) bond priced at 90.165:

Current yield = $\dfrac{8}{90.165}$ = 8.873%   YTM = 12%

- Current yield *ignores movement toward par value*
- Current yield < YTM for discount bond
- Current yield > YTM for premium bond

Simple Yield

Simple yield assumes straight-line amortization of premium or discount.

Simple yield = $\dfrac{\text{annual coupon payment} \pm \text{amortization}}{\text{flat price}}$

8% 3-year semiannual-pay bond priced at 90.165:

Discount = 9.835; 9.835 / 3 = 3.278

Simple yield = $\dfrac{8 + 3.278}{90.165}$ = 12.51%

Yield Conventions

Street convention assumes payments are made on scheduled dates.

True yield uses actual payment dates, taking account of holidays and weekends.

Government equivalent yield: Corporate bond yield restated based on 365-day year; used for calculating spread to benchmark government bond yield.

LOS 53.f Calculate/Interpret
CFAI p. 416, Schweser p. 42

Introduction to
Fixed-Income Valuation

Yield-to-Call (YTC)

Yield-to-first-call: Substitute the call price at the first call date for par and number of periods to the first call date for N.

Different YTC for each of a bond's call dates and prices.

Yield-to-worst is the lowest of YTM and the YTCs for all the call dates and prices.

© Kaplan, Inc.

60

LOS 53.f Calculate/Interpret
CFAI p. 416, Schweser p. 42

Introduction to
Fixed-Income Valuation

10-year, 5% semiannual bond priced at 102.8

1. What is the YTM on a semiannual bond basis?

2. If it is callable in two years at 101, what is the YTC?

© Kaplan, Inc.

61-5

LOS 53.f Calculate/Interpret
CFAI p. 416, Schweser p. 42

Introduction to
Fixed-Income Valuation

Option-Adjusted Yield

More precise yield measure for callable bonds:

1. **Value the call option using a pricing model and expected yield volatility**

2. **Add the call option value to the bond price**

3. **Calculate the option-adjusted yield based on the option-adjusted price**

For putable bond, subtract the value of the put option to get option-adjusted price.

© Kaplan, Inc.

62

LOS 53.f Calculate/Interpret
CFAI p. 416, Schweser p. 42

Introduction to
Fixed-Income Valuation

Floating-Rate Notes

Coupon at next reset date = reference rate at previous reset date ± quoted margin

Required margin (discount margin) is the margin that would cause the note's value to return to par at the reset date; may differ from quoted margin if issuer's credit quality changes

- If required margin > quoted margin, price < par at reset date
- If required margin < quoted margin, price > par at reset date

© Kaplan, Inc.

63

Money Market Instruments

- Yields quoted as simple annual interest
- May be discount or add-on yields
- May use 360-day or 365-day year
- Compare money market instruments based on **bond equivalent yield**—add-on yield based on 365-day year
  - Treat periodicity of yield as 365/days to maturity

© Kaplan, Inc.

64

Bond Equivalent Yield

Calculate BEY for a $1,000 note with 219 days to maturity and an annualized discount of 2% based on a 360-day year.

Discount = 2% × 219 / 360 × $1,000 = $12.17

Current price = $1,000 − $12.17 = $987.83

HPR = $12.17 / $987.83 = 1.23%

BEY = 1.23% × 365 / 219 = 2.05%

© Kaplan, Inc.

65 - 4

Yield Curves

A **yield curve** or **term structure** shows yields for bonds at different maturities.

Ideally, the bonds would have the same:

- Currency denomination
- Credit risk
- Liquidity
- Coupon rate/reinvestment risk
- Tax treatment
- Periodicity and yield calculation method

© Kaplan, Inc.

66

Yield Curves

Spot (Zero) Yield Curve

YTM of government zeros

Same currency, credit risk, liquidity, tax treatment, and coupon rate/reinvestment risk

However, not actively traded across all maturities so yield curves are constructed using coupon bond yields

© Kaplan, Inc.

67

Yield Curves

Coupon Bond Yield Curve

Semiannual bonds issued for specific maturities (e.g., for 1, 3, 5, 7, 10 years)

- Newly issued bonds are close to par (similar tax effects), actively traded (similar liquidity)
- Other maturities based on linear interpolation
- Yields for 1-, 3-, 6-, and 12-month maturities often must be converted from discount basis to semiannual bond equivalent yields

© Kaplan, Inc.

68

Yield Curves

Par Curve

What coupon would a bond at each maturity need to pay to be priced at par?

$$100 = \frac{PMT}{1+Z_1} + \frac{PMT}{(1+Z_2)^2} + \frac{PMT}{(1+Z_3)^3} + \ldots + \frac{100+PMT}{(1+Z_N)^N}$$

Use spot rates for each maturity to solve for PMT

The **forward yield curve** shows rates for future periods (e.g., the 1-year rate one, two, and three years from now).

© Kaplan, Inc.

69

Forward Rates

N-period rates at some date in the future:

- **1y1y** is the 1-year rate, one year from now
- **2y1y** is the *1-year* rate, *two* years from now
- **1y2y** is the 2-year rate, *one* year from now
- **2y3y** is the 3-year rate, *two* years from now
- **S_N** is the N-year spot rate (also Z_N)

All are expressed as annualized rates

© Kaplan, Inc.

70

Implied **Forward Rates**

$$(1 + S_3)^3 = (1 + S_1)(1 + 1y1y)(1 + 2y1y)$$

$$(1 + S_3)^3 = (1 + S_1)(1 + 1y2y)^2$$

$$(1 + S_3)^3 = (1 + S_2)^2(1 + 2y1y)$$

Cost of borrowing for three years at S_3 should equal cost of:

- Borrowing for one year at S_1, one year at 1y1y, and one year at 2y1y
- Borrowing for one year at S_1 and for two years at 1y2y
- Borrowing for two years at S_2 and for one year at 2y1y

© Kaplan, Inc.

71

Introduction to
Fixed-Income Valuation

Forward Rates From Spot Rates

$S_2 = 4\%$, $S_4 = 5\%$, calculate 2y2y.

$$\sqrt{\frac{(1+S_4)^4}{(1+S_2)^2}} - 1 = 2y2y,\ \text{so}\ \sqrt{\frac{(1.05)^4}{(1.04)^2}} - 1 = 6.01\%$$

Approximation: $4 \times 5\% - 2 \times 4\% = 20\% - 8\% = 12\%$

$12\% / 2 = 6\%$

To get 2y2y as annual rate, we take the square root (or divide by two for the approximation).

© Kaplan, Inc.   73

Introduction to
Fixed-Income Valuation

Valuing a Bond With Forward Rates

1-year rate is 3.0%; 1y1y = 3.5%; 2y1y = 4.0%

Value a 4%, 3-year annual-pay bond:

$$\frac{40}{1.03} + \frac{40}{(1.03)(1.035)} + \frac{1040}{(1.03)(1.035)(1.04)} = 1{,}014.40$$

$$1+S_1 \qquad (1+S_2)^2 \qquad (1+S_3)^3$$

© Kaplan, Inc.   75

Introduction to
Fixed-Income Valuation

Forward Rates From Spot Rates

$S_2 = 4\%$, $S_3 = 5\%$, calculate 2y1y

$$\frac{(1+S_3)^3}{(1+S_2)^2} - 1 = 2y1y,\ \text{so}\ \frac{(1.05)^3}{(1.04)^2} - 1 = 7.03\%$$

Approximation: $3 \times 5\% - 2 \times 4\% = 15\% - 8\% = 7\%$

© Kaplan, Inc.   72

Introduction to
Fixed-Income Valuation

Spot Rates From Forward Rates

Spot rate is geometric mean of forward rates:

$$[(1+S_1)(1+1y1y)(1+2y1y)]^{\frac{1}{3}} - 1 = S_3$$

Example: $S_1 = 4.0\%$, 1y1y = 5.0%, 2y1y = 5.5%

3-period spot rate =

$$[(1.04)(1.05)(1.055)]^{\frac{1}{3}} - 1 = S_3 = 4.8314\%$$

Approximation: $(4+5+5.5)/3 = 4.833$

© Kaplan, Inc.   74

Current 1-year spot rate is 6%, 2-year spot rate is 7%, and 3-year spot rate is 6%. The 1-year forward rate for a loan two years from now is *closest* to:

A. 6%.

B. 5%.

C. 4%.

Yield Spreads

Allow the separation of changes in *risk-free* rates from changes in yield premiums for credit risk, liquidity, and other bond differences.

RFR driven by macroeconomic factors

Spreads driven by microeconomic factors

G-Spread: Spread is to benchmark government bond yield for same maturity (U.S., U.K., Japan).

On-the-run bond yields or interpolated yields

Yield Spreads

For eurozone bonds, spreads are relative to swap rates, the fixed rate of a fixed-for-floating swap.

For example, a 5-year corporate euro coupon bond might be quoted as "mid-swap +80 bp."

This spread represents the credit risk difference between interbank lending (Libor) and the bond.

These spreads are termed **I-spreads** (for interpolated spreads).

Yield Spreads

Z-spreads (static spreads) are the amount added to each spot rate (government or swap) to get the bond price.

$$Price = \frac{PMT}{1+Z_1+Z} + \frac{PMT}{(1+Z_2+Z)^2} + \frac{PMT}{(1+Z_3+Z)^3} + \cdots + \frac{100+PMT}{(1+Z_N+Z)^N}$$

Option-adjusted spread (OAS)

= Z-spread – option value in basis points per year (e.g., 10-year callable bond has Z-spread of 180 bp)

Call option increases yield 60 bp

OAS = 180 − 60 = 120 bp

CFA Curriculum Vol. 5,
R.53, Q.31, p. 450

**Introduction to
Fixed-Income Valuation**

A two-year floating-rate note pays 6-month Libor plus 80 basis points. The floater is priced at 97 per 100 of par value. Current 6-month Libor is 1.00%. Assume a 30/360 day-count convention and evenly spaced periods. The discount margin for the floater in basis points (bps) is *closest* to:

A. 180 bps.

B. 236 bps.

C. 420 bps.

81 - 3

LOS 54.a Explain
CFAI p. 470, Schweser p. 71

**Introduction to
Asset-Backed Securities**

Benefits of Securitization

Reduces funding costs for firms that securitize financial assets

Increases liquidity for the financial assets

Offers investors exposure to new asset classes

83

CFA Curriculum Vol. 5,
R.53, Q.26, p. 449

**Introduction to
Fixed-Income Valuation**

A 5-year, 5% semiannual coupon payment corporate bond is priced at 104.967 per 100 of par value. The bond's yield-to-maturity, quoted on a semiannual bond basis, is 3.897%. An analyst has been asked to convert to a monthly periodicity. Under this conversion, the yield-to-maturity is *closest to*:

A. 3.87%.

B. 4.95%.

C. 7.67%.

80 - 1

Fixed Income

Fixed Income:
Basic Concepts

54. Introduction to
Asset-Backed Securities

KAPLAN UNIVERSITY | SCHOOL OF PROFESSIONAL AND CONTINUING EDUCATION | **SCHWESER**

Asset Securitization Process

Seller: Originates assets and sells to issuer

Issuer/Special Purpose Entity (SPE): Sells ABS; buys assets

Investors: Buy securities; receive cash flows

Servicer: Collects payments (often the seller)

Example: Asset Securitization

Asset Securitization Process

- The SPE is **bankruptcy remote** from the seller

  - ABS issued by the SPE may have a higher credit rating than bonds issued by the seller

  - Lower cost of funds with securitization than by issuing corporate bonds

---

Structures of Securitizations

Two basic securitization structures (can have both):

- **Senior/subordinated structure** (credit tranching)

  Subordinated bonds absorb credit losses first

  Also termed *waterfall structure*

- **Sequential structure** (time tranching)

  First bond class receives all principal payments and prepayments until paid off, then second class.......

Residential Mortgage Loans

Loans with residential real estate as collateral

Loan-to-value ratio (LTV): Percentage of collateral value that is borrowed

Lower LTV → lower probability of default, greater recovery percentage

© Kaplan, Inc.

88

Mortgage Characteristics

- **Maturity:** Typically 15–30 years in U.S., 20–40 years in Europe, up to 100 years in Japan

- **Interest rate:** Fixed, adjustable (ARM), convertible between fixed and adjustable

- **Amortization:** Full, partial, interest-only

- **Prepayment** provisions: May have penalty

- **Recourse** or **nonrecourse** loans: Possibility of strategic default on nonrecourse loans

© Kaplan, Inc.

89

Residential Mortgage-Backed Securities (RMBS)

Agency RMBS: Issued by government agency (e.g., GNMA) or government-sponsored enterprise (e.g., FNMA, FHLMC)

Only **conforming loans** may be included in agency RMBS

Nonagency RMBS: Issued by private entities; underlying loans do not have government backing

Nonagency RMBS have more credit risk and therefore need credit enhancement

© Kaplan, Inc.

90

Mortgage Pass-through Securities

Securitization: Pool mortgages to diversify risk

Investors receive a pro rata share of all cash flows

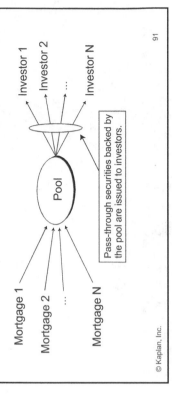

© Kaplan, Inc.

91

Mortgage Pass-through Securities

Weighted average maturity (WAM): Maturities weighted by outstanding principal of mortgages in pool

Weighted average coupon (WAC): Interest rates weighted by outstanding principal of mortgages in pool

© Kaplan, Inc.

92

Nonagency RMBS

External credit enhancements

1. Corporate guarantee by seller

2. Bank letter of credit

3. Bond insurance

© Kaplan, Inc.

93

Nonagency RMBS

Internal credit enhancements

1. Reserve funds
   - Cash reserve funds
   - Excess servicing spread funds

2. Overcollateralization
   - Face value < underlying collateral value
   - Excess used to absorb losses

3. Senior/subordinated structure
   - Subordinated tranches absorb losses first
   - Shifting interest mechanism: Prepayments change protection by subordinated tranches

© Kaplan, Inc.

94

Collateralized Mortgage Obligations

CMOs: Created from pass-through MBS (the *collateral*) for investors with different risk needs

- Cash flows reallocated to different tranches, each with different contraction/extension risk

- Risks can be reallocated, but not eliminated

- Two typical structures:

   1. Sequential pay structure

   2. PAC/support structure

© Kaplan, Inc.

95

Collateralized Mortgage Obligations

Sequential pay CMO

- All tranches receive interest
- Shortest tranche receives all principal until paid off
- Each sequential pay CMO tranche has mix of contraction and extension risk

© Kaplan, Inc.

96

Sequential Pay CMO

Tranche	Contraction Risk	Extension Risk
A (sequential pay)	HIGH	LOW
B (sequential pay)		
C (sequential pay)		
D (sequential pay)	LOW	HIGH

© Kaplan, Inc.

97

Collateralized Mortgage Obligations

Planned Amortization Class (PAC) CMO structure

PAC tranche

- Scheduled principal payments within range of two prepayment rates (called the **initial PAC collar**)
- PAC tranche has more predictable cash flows and average life

Support tranche

- Provides prepayment protection to PAC tranches

© Kaplan, Inc.

98

Planned Amortization Class CMO

Average Life Variability Effective collar: 100 to 300 PSA		
PSA Speed	PAC I Tranche	Support Tranche
50	8.8 years	21.1 years
100	6.5	17.1
200	6.5	10.4
300	6.5	2.9
400	5.4	1.8
500	4.2	1.2

© Kaplan, Inc.

99

Collateralized Mortgage Obligations

Relative to PAC, support tranche has more:

Extension risk: When prepayments fall, support tranche average life increases by more than PAC

Contraction risk: When prepayments increase, support tranche average life decreases by more than PAC

© Kaplan, Inc.

100

Which of the following describes a typical feature of a non-agency residential mortgage-backed security (RMBS)?

A. Senior/subordinated structure.

B. A pool of conforming mortgages as collateral.

C. A guarantee by a government-sponsored enterprise.

101 – 1

Prepayment Risk

Characteristics of mortgage pool change due to prepayments, which depend on level and path of interest rates

Contraction risk: Interest rates decrease, prepayments increase

- Lower rates lead to more refinancing
- More refinancing shortens average MBS life

Extension risk: Interest rates increase, prepayments decrease → longer average MBS life

© Kaplan, Inc.

102

Prepayment Risk

Single monthly mortality rate (SMM): Percentage by which prepayments reduce principal balance, compared to no prepayments

Conditional prepayment rate (CPR): Annualized prepayment rate, based on WAC, interest rates, prior prepayments

Weighted average life: Less than WAM because of prepayments

© Kaplan, Inc.

103

Prepayment Risk

Public Securities Association (PSA) prepayment benchmark

- Monthly series of annual prepayment rates
- Assumes monthly prepayment rate increases as pool ages

100 PSA = 100% of PSA

200 PSA = 2 × (CPR of 100 PSA)

In the context of mortgage-backed securities, a conditional prepayment rate (CPR) of 8% means that approximately 8% of an outstanding mortgage pool balance at the beginning of the year will be prepaid:

A. in the current month.

B. by the end of the year.

C. over the life of the mortgages.

Commercial MBS

Commercial mortgages: Nonrecourse loans, partially amortizing

Balloon risk → extension risk for CMBS

Analysis focuses on risk of property:

- **Debt service coverage ratio**

  = NOI / debt service

- **Loan-to-value ratio**

  = mortgage / appraised value

CMBS: Call Protection

Call protection—two sources:

Loan-level:

- Prepayment lockout (two to five years)
- Defeasance
- Prepayment penalty points
- Yield maintenance charges

CMBS structure:

  Sequential tranches

Credit Card ABS

- Backed by **pool of credit card receivables**

- **Nonamortizing** loans

- **Lockout period**
  - No principal repaid
    - Principal payments by card holders used to purchase more receivables

- **Early (rapid) amortization provisions** and **senior/subordinate structure** are typically included

© Kaplan, Inc.

109

Collateralized Debt Obligations

Typical CDO structure:

- **Senior tranches:** 70–80% of total, floating rate

- **Mezzanine tranches:** Fixed coupon

- **Equity (subordinated) tranche:** Provides prepayment and credit protection

© Kaplan, Inc.

111

Auto Loan ABS

Amortizing loans—Prepayments may result from:

- Sold/traded-in/paid early

- Wrecked/stolen, loan prepaid with insurance proceeds

ABS needs credit enhancement, due to risk of default

© Kaplan, Inc.

108

Collateralized Debt Obligations (CDOs)

Collateral is a **pool of debt obligations**

- Corporate, emerging market bonds (CBOs)

- Leveraged bank loans (CLOs)

- MBS and ABS (structured finance CDOs)

Collateral pool is **managed** to generate cash flows to make promised payments

© Kaplan, Inc.

110

Fixed Income

Additional Problems

Additional Problems

2) Given the following bond information:

Coupon rate = 6%, Payment dates: Jan. 2 and July 2
Maturity: Jan. 2, 2030, YTM = 7%, Day count = 30/360.
A trade for the bond will require a payment at settlement on Aug. 23, 2014, that is:

A. equal to 91.50.

B. less than 91.50.

C. greater than 91.50.

Collateralized Debt Obligations

Synthetic CDOs: Take on economic risks (but not legal ownership) of underlying assets using a **credit default swap** rather than a cash market position

Arbitrage CDOs: Generate return on spread between collateral interest and funding costs

---

Additional Problems

1) Given the following Eurodollar forward rates:

$S_1 = 6.45\%$, 1y1y = 6.15%, 2y1y = 5.90%

What is the value of a 3-year, annual-pay 6% coupon Eurodollar bond?

A. 98.81.

B. 99.53.

C. 100.21.

Additional Problems

3) An interpolated spread (I-spread) is calculated relative to:

A. a swap fixed rate.

B. the benchmark spot rate curve.

C. a benchmark government bond yield.

- 1

Additional Problems

4) An investor is considering purchasing one of the following three 5-year bonds:

Bond	Interest	Coupon	Price
A	Semiannual	6.50%	98.54
B	Annual	6.25%	97.33
C	Monthly	6.35%	97.72

Which bond has the highest effective yield?

- 7

STUDY SESSION 15 ANSWERS

Reading	Slide Number	Answer
51	16	B
51	19	B
53	39	$901.65
53	40	A
53	46(1)	86.410
53	46(2)	87.341
53	46(3)	88.348
53	56	A
53	61(1)	4.646%
53	61(2)	4.014%
53	76	C
53	80	A
54	101	A
54	105	B

Additional Problems

1. B

2. C

3. A

4. Bond C

Study Session 16

Fixed Income: Analysis of Risk

Fixed Income: Analysis of Risk

55. Understanding Fixed-Income Risk and Return

Study Session 16
Fixed Income: Analysis of Risk

55. Understanding Fixed-Income Risk and Return
56. Fundamentals of Credit Analysis

CFA Curriculum Vol. 5,
R.55, Q.2, p. 575

Which of the following sources of return is *most likely* exposed to interest rate risk for an investor of a fixed-rate bond who holds the bond until maturity?
A.   Capital gain or loss.
B.   Redemption of principal.
C.   Reinvestment of coupon payments.

3 – 1

LOS 55.a Calculate/Interpret
CFAI p. 526, Schweser p. 94

Sources of Bond Return

Coupon and principal payments

Reinvestment of coupon payments
　　Assume reinvestment rate = YTM

Capital gain or loss
- Relative to *constant-yield price trajectory*
- Zero if held to maturity

2

Calculating Bond Returns

3-year bond, 6% annual coupon, YTM = 7%, Price = 97.376, held to maturity (no capital gains/loss)

Principal and interest $6 + 6 + 6 + 100 = 118$

Reinvestment income

$6(1.07)^2 + 6(1.07) + 6 - 3(6) = 1.29$

Realized return $\left(\dfrac{118+1.29}{97.376}\right)^{\frac{1}{3}} - 1 = 7\% = $ YTM at purchase

4

George Sanchez, CFA, just bought a 10-year, 9% coupon, semiannual-pay, U.S. corporate at 101.50. If he is able to reinvest coupon income at 6% over the life of the bonds, his realized 10-year return (w/semiannual compounding) will be:

A. 3.97%.

B. 6.36%.

C. 7.93%.

5 - 3

Calculating Capital Gain

Capital gain (loss) = sale price – carrying value

Carrying value based on constant YTM

20-year bond, 5% semiannual coupon, purchased at YTM of 6% (price = 88.4426), sold after 5 years for 91.40

Carrying value: N = 15 × 2 = 30; I/Y = 6 / 2 = 3; PMT = 5 / 2 = 2.5; FV = 100; CPT→PV = –90.20

Capital gain = 91.40 – 90.20 = 1.20% of par value

6

A 30-year, 4% coupon, semiannual-pay bond purchased at a YTM of 5% is sold after 5 years for 87.52. The capital gain or loss on the bond sale per 100 of face value is *closest* to:

A. 1.60.

B. 1.70.

C. 1.80.

7 - 2

Effect of Change in YTM

YTM changes after purchase but just prior to the first coupon date, coupon reinvestment rate = YTM

Case #1: Bond held to maturity

$$\text{Rate of return} = \left(\frac{\text{Coupons} + \text{Par} + \text{Reinvestment income}}{\text{Purchase cost}}\right)^{\frac{1}{N}} - 1$$

Only reinvestment income is affected:

YTM ↑   Reinvestment rate ↑   Realized return ↑
YTM ↓   Reinvestment rate ↓   Realized return ↓

Reinvestment risk greater than price risk

© Kaplan, Inc.   8

Effect of Change in YTM

YTM changes after purchase but just prior to the first coupon date, coupon reinvestment rate = YTM

Case #2: Bond sold after one period

$$\text{Rate of return} = \left(\frac{\text{Coupon} + \text{Sale price}}{\text{Purchase cost}}\right) - 1$$

Only sale price is affected:

YTM ↑   Sale price ↓   Realized return ↓
YTM ↓   Sale price↑   Realized return ↑

Price risk greater than reinvestment risk

© Kaplan, Inc.   9

Macaulay Duration

Weighted average of periods until cash flows are paid, weights are proportion of total present value

3-year annual-pay 4% bond, YTM = 5%

Cash flow	PV of cash flow	Weight
40	$40 / 1.05 = 38.10$	$38.10 / 972.77 = 3.92\%$
40	$40 / 1.05^2 = 36.28$	$36.28 / 972.77 = 3.73\%$
1,040	$1,040 / 1.05^3 = 898.39$	$898.39 / 972.77 = 92.35\%$
	972.77	100%

MacDur = 1(0.0392) + 2(0.0373) + 3(0.9235)
= 2.8843 years

© Kaplan, Inc.   10

Macaulay Duration

3-year semiannual-pay 4% bond, YTM = 5%

Cash flow	PV of cash flow	Weight
20	$20 / 1.025 = 19.51$	$19.51 / 972.46 = 0.0201$
20	$20 / 1.025^2 = 19.04$	$19.04 / 972.46 = 0.0196$
20	$20 / 1.025^3 = 18.57$	$18.57 / 972.46 = 0.0191$
20	$20 / 1.025^4 = 18.12$	$18.12 / 972.46 = 0.0186$
20	$20 / 1.025^5 = 17.68$	$17.68 / 972.46 = 0.0182$
1,020	$1,020 / 1.025^6 = 879.54$	$879.54 / 972.46 = 0.9044$
	972.46	1.0000

MacDur = 1(0.0201) + 2(0.0196) + 3(0.0191) + 4(0.0186) +
5(0.0182) + 6(0.9044) = 5.7084 ÷ 2 = 2.8542 years

© Kaplan, Inc.   11

Modified Duration

Approximate percentage price change for a 1% change in yield:

$$ModDur_{ANNUAL} = MacDur_{ANNUAL} / (1 + YTM)$$

Approximate modified duration:

$$\frac{\text{price w/YTM} \downarrow - \text{price w/YTM} \uparrow}{2 \times \text{initial price} \times \Delta YTM}$$

© Kaplan, Inc.

12

Consider a bond trading at a full price of 980:

YTM increases 0.5%, full price decreases to 960

YTM down by 0.5%, full price increases to 1,002

The approximate modified duration is:

A. equal to 4.4.

B. greater than 4.4.

C. less than 4.4.

© Kaplan, Inc.

13 - 1

Effective Duration

- Must be used for bonds with embedded options because their cash flows depend on interest rate levels and paths
- Not necessarily better for small changes in yield

Based on:

1. Parallel shift in benchmark yield curve
2. Pricing model for bonds with embedded options

$$\frac{\text{price w/curve decrease} - \text{price w/curve increase}}{2 \times \text{initial price} \times \text{decimal change in curve}}$$

© Kaplan, Inc.

14

Key Rate Duration

- Macaulay, modified, or effective duration measures price sensitivity to a parallel shift in yield curve
- **Key rate duration** (or **partial duration**) measures price sensitivity to a change in yield for a specific maturity
- Key rate durations may be used to estimate effect on bond prices of change in the shape of the yield curve (e.g., steepening or flattening)

© Kaplan, Inc.

15

Slide 16

LOS 55.e Explain
CFAI p. 545, Schweser p. 105

Understanding Fixed-Income
Risk and Return

Factors Affecting Duration

With other factors unchanged:

Longer maturity → **higher** duration
(except for some discount bonds)

Higher coupon rate → **lower** duration

Higher YTM → **lower** duration

© Kaplan, Inc.

16

Slide 17

LOS 55.e Explain
CFAI p. 545, Schweser p. 105

Understanding Fixed-Income
Risk and Return

Factors Affecting Duration

12-year, 6% annual-pay par bond

Macaulay duration = 8.89 years

© Kaplan, Inc.

17

Slide 18

Understanding Fixed-Income
Risk and Return

Other things equal, which of the following bonds has the *least* interest rate risk?

A. 10-year, Baa rated, 8% coupon, noncallable bond trading at 108.

B. 10-year, A rated, zero-coupon, noncallable bond trading at 50.83.

C. 25-year, 6% Treasury bond trading at par.

© Kaplan, Inc.

18 - 3

Slide 19

LOS 55.f Calculate/Explain
CFAI p. 551, Schweser p. 106

Understanding Fixed-Income
Risk and Return

Portfolio Duration Measures

Method #1: Weighted average number of periods until portfolio cash flows are due to be received

- Theoretically correct but rarely used
- Based on cash flow yield, IRR of portfolio cash flows
- Cannot be used if bonds have embedded options

Method #2: Weighted average of bonds' durations

- May be used with effective durations
- Assumes parallel shifts in yield curve

© Kaplan, Inc.

19

Price Value of a Basis Point

Change in full price for a 1 bp change in YTM

PVBP Example:

10-year, 5% annual-pay bond, @par = $100,000

Value at YTM of 4.99% = 100,077.25 (+77.25)

Value at YTM of 5.01% = 99,922.82 (−77.18)

         Difference =   154.43

PVBP = 154.43 / 2 = $77.22

21

Money Duration

Money duration = ModDur$_{ANNUAL}$ × full price

Money duration for a bond with a full price of $1,350,871 and a modified duration of 8.35.

8.35 × $1,350,871 = $11,279,772.85

Change in full price for an increase in yield of 0.007

−0.007 × 11,279,772.85 = decrease of $78,958

Money duration per 100 of par value

= ModDur$_{ANNUAL}$ × full price per 100 of par value

20

Approximate and Effective Convexity

Approximate convexity assumes expected cash flows do not change when yield changes.

Effective convexity takes into account changes in cash flows due to embedded options, while approximate convexity does not.

Bondholders prefer more convexity, other things equal.

23

The Convexity Adjustment

Duration-based estimates of bond prices are below actual prices for option-free bonds

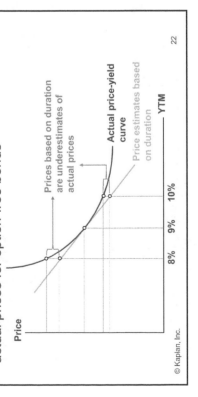

22

LOS 55.h Calculate/Interpret/Distinguish   Understanding Fixed-Income
CFAI p. 555, Schweser p. 108   Risk and Return

Approximate and Effective Convexity

Approximate convexity:

$$\frac{V_- + V_+ - 2V_0}{(\Delta YTM)^2 \times V_0}$$

Approximate effective convexity:

$$\frac{V_- + V_+ - 2V_0}{(\Delta curve)^2 \times V_0}$$

© Kaplan, Inc.   24

LOS 55.h Calculate/Interpret/Distinguish   Understanding Fixed-Income
CFAI p. 555, Schweser p. 108   Risk and Return

Price-Yield for Callable Bond

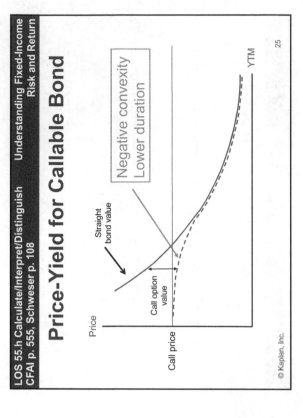

© Kaplan, Inc.   25

LOS 55.h Calculate/Interpret/Distinguish   Understanding Fixed-Income
CFAI p. 555, Schweser p. 108   Risk and Return

Price-Yield for Putable Bond

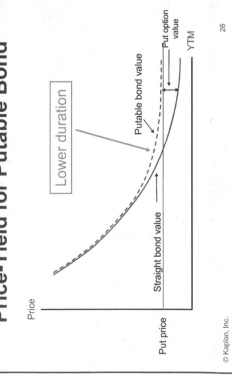

© Kaplan, Inc.   26

LOS 55.i Estimate   Understanding Fixed-Income
CFAI p. 555, Schweser p. 111   Risk and Return

Using Duration and Convexity

$\Delta Price \approx -ModDur(\Delta YTM) + \frac{1}{2} ApproxCon (\Delta YTM)^2$

Bond has: ModDur = 7.5   ApproxCon = 130

For a 25 bp **increase** in YTM:

Duration effect	$-7.5(0.0025)$	$= -0.0188$
Convexity effect	$(\frac{1}{2})(130)(0.0025)^2$	$= 0.0004$
$\Delta Price$		$= -1.84\%$

25 bp **decrease** in YTM: +0.0188 + 0.0004 = **+1.92%**

© Kaplan, Inc.   27

Term Structure of Yield Volatility

YTM volatility and time-to-maturity relationship

Short-term rates driven by monetary policy

Long-term rates driven by E[inflation] and E[growth]: Short-term YTM may be more volatile than long-term YTM so that term structure of yield volatility slopes downward.

Bond with lower duration may have higher volatility of YTM so price volatility is higher

Yield curve shifts are not necessarily parallel

© Kaplan, Inc.

28

Duration and Investment Horizon

Macaulay duration = investment horizon at which price risk and reinvestment risk just offset

Duration gap = MacDur − investment horizon

> 0: Increase in YTM decreases returns

< 0: Decrease in YTM decreases returns

© Kaplan, Inc.

29

An investor purchases an annual coupon bond with a 6% coupon rate and exactly 20 years remaining until maturity at a price equal to par value. The investor's investment horizon is eight years. The approximate modified duration of the bond is 11.470 years. The duration gap at the time of purchase is *closest* to:

A. −7.842.

B. 3.470.

C. 4.158.

30 - 2

Credit Spreads and Liquidity

Benchmark yield composed of real risk-free rate and expected inflation

Spread to benchmark includes premiums for **credit risk** and **illiquidity**

Estimate price effect of change in spread using duration and convexity (same as for ΔYTM) :

$$-\text{duration}(\Delta\text{spread}) + 1/2 \text{ convexity}(\Delta\text{spread})^2$$

© Kaplan, Inc.

31

Slide 1 (title slide)

Fixed Income: Analysis of Risk

56. Fundamentals of Credit Analysis

KAPLAN UNIVERSITY | SCHOOL OF PROFESSIONAL AND CONTINUING EDUCATION | SCHWESER

Slide 33

LOS 56.a,b Describe
CFAI p. 588, Schweser p. 124

Credit-Related Risks

Credit risk: Risk of losses if borrower fails to pay interest or principal

Default risk: Probability of default

Loss severity: Amount or percentage of principal and interest lost if borrower defaults

Expected loss = default risk × loss severity

Recovery rate = 1 – loss severity in %

© Kaplan, Inc.

33

Slide 34

LOS 56.a Describe
CFAI p. 588, Schweser p. 124

Credit-Related Risks

Spread risk: Risk of spread widening, primarily from

Credit migration (downgrade) risk: Issuer becomes less creditworthy, bond rating falls

Market liquidity risk: Receive less than market value when selling bond, increases required yield spread

© Kaplan, Inc.

34

Slide 35

LOS 56.c Describe/Explain
CFAI p. 591, Schweser p. 125

Seniority Ranking

Different bonds from same issuer may have different **seniority** or priority of claims

- First lien/mortgage > second lien/mortgage
- Secured > unsecured
- Senior > junior > subordinated
- Issues may combine these features
  e.g., senior secured > junior secured

All debt in same category ranks **pari passu** (has same priority of claims)

© Kaplan, Inc.

35

Priority of Claims in Bankruptcy

Priority of claims is not always followed strictly in bankruptcy

- Creditors may negotiate different outcome to limit delays and bankruptcy-related costs to issuing firm

  - Bankruptcy court may order different outcome

© Kaplan, Inc.

36

Credit Ratings

Rating agencies: Moody's, S&P, Fitch

Corporate family rating (CFR): Issuer credit rating, applies to senior <u>unsecured</u> debt

Corporate credit rating (CCR): Applies to specific debt issue; may be **notched** up or down from CFR

© Kaplan, Inc.

37

Credit Ratings

Investment Grade

Moody's	S&P, Fitch
Aaa	AAA
Aa1	AA+
Aa2	AA
Aa3	AA–
A1	A+
A2	A
A3	A–
Baa1	BBB+
Baa2	BBB
Baa3	BBB–

Non-Investment Grade

Moody's	S&P, Fitch	Moody's	S&P, Fitch
Ba1	BB+	Caa1	CCC+
Ba2	BB	Caa2	CCC
Ba3	BB–	Caa3	CCC–
B1	B+	Ca	CC
B2	B	C	C
B3	B–	C	D

In default

© Kaplan, Inc.

38

Topper, Inc. has a CFR of Ba2. Topper's subordinated debentures are *least likely* to be rated:

A. Ba1.

B. Ba2.

C. Ba3.

© Kaplan, Inc.

39 - 1

LOS 56.e Explain
CFAI p. 601, Schweser p. 127

Risks in Relying on Credit Ratings

- Credit rating may change: Downgrade, upgrade
- Rating agencies make mistakes (subprime mortgages)
- Issuer-specific risks may be unpredictable (litigation, natural disasters, leveraged buyouts)
- Prices/spreads adjust faster than credit ratings

Ratings reflect default risk
Spreads reflect <u>expected loss</u>

© Kaplan, Inc.

40

LOS 56.f Explain
CFAI p. 607, Schweser p. 128

Four Cs of Credit Analysis

Capacity: Ability to pay on time and in full, industry structure/competition, industry and company fundamentals

Collateral: Value of assets, depreciation/book value, intangible assets that can be sold

Covenants: Legal stipulations of bond issue

Character: Management integrity, history, accounting, treatment of debtholders vs. equity

© Kaplan, Inc.

41

LOS 56.g Calculate/Interpret
CFAI p. 611, Schweser p. 130

Financial Ratios in Credit Analysis

Credit analysts focus on **leverage ratios** and **coverage ratios**

Profit and cash flow metrics:
- EBITDA, EBIT
- Funds from operations (FFO), net income from continuing operations adjusted for non-cash items
- Free cash flow before/after dividends

© Kaplan, Inc.

42

LOS 56.g Calculate/Interpret
CFAI p. 611, Schweser p. 130

Leverage Ratios

- Higher leverage → higher credit risk
- Adjust debt to include all obligations (underfunded pensions, off-balance-sheet liabilities, DTLs expected to reverse)

Debt-to-capital, debt-to-EBITDA:
  - Higher ratio → higher leverage
  - May adjust capital for writedown of goodwill

FFO-to-debt: Higher ratio → lower leverage

© Kaplan, Inc.

43

Coverage Ratios

Measure earnings relative to interest obligations

Higher coverage → lower credit risk

EBITDA-to-interest expense

EBIT-to-interest expense: More conservative

© Kaplan, Inc. 44

Example: Credit Quality

	York, Inc.	Zale, Inc.	Industry Average
EBIT	$550	$2,250	$1,400
FFO	$300	$850	$600
Interest expense	$40	$160	$100
Total debt	$1,000	$2,500	$2,400
Total capital	$4,000	$6,500	$6,000

- York has goodwill of $500 and operating lease obligations with a present value of $900.
- Zale has a net pension liability of $200 and no operating leases.
- Industry averages are goodwill of $200, PV of operating leases of $200, and no net pension asset or liability.

© Kaplan, Inc. 45

Example: Credit Quality

Recommended analyst adjustments:

- Include operating lease obligations, net pension liabilities in total debt
- Calculate debt-to-capital ratios with and without goodwill

	York, Inc.	Zale, Inc.	Industry Average
EBIT	$550	$2,250	$1,400
FFO	$300	$850	$600
Interest expense	$40	$160	$100
Total debt	$1,900 ($3,500)	$2,700	$2,600
Total capital	$4,000 ($3,500)	$6,500	$6,000 ($5,800)

© Kaplan, Inc. 46

Example: Credit Quality

	York, Inc.	Zale, Inc.	Industry Average
EBIT / interest	13.8×	14.1×	14.0×
FFO / debt	15.8%	31.5%	23.1%
Debt / capital	47.5% (54.3%)	41.5%	43.3% (44.8%)

- York and Zale have interest coverage (EBIT / interest) in line with their industry average.
- Adjusting for all obligations, York is more leveraged (lower FFO/debt, higher debt/capital) than Zale and the industry average; Zale is less leveraged than the industry average.
- Therefore, Zale appears more creditworthy than York.

© Kaplan, Inc. 47

Yield Spreads: Level and Volatility

Yield spread = credit spread + liquidity premium

Spreads seem to be more volatile for lower-quality bonds than for higher-quality bonds

Factors affecting yield spreads:

- Credit cycle
- Economic conditions
- Market performance, including equities
- Broker/dealer capital
- Supply of new issues

© Kaplan, Inc.

48

Additional Learning Outcomes

LOS 56.j: high-yield, sovereign, municipal debt

© Kaplan, Inc.

49

Additional Problems

KAPLAN
UNIVERSITY SCHOOL OF PROFESSIONAL
AND CONTINUING EDUCATION | SCHWESER

1) Jack is considering purchasing a bond that is currently priced at 85.50. After performing a scenario analysis, Jack computed the following prices for the bond for 50 bp shifts in the benchmark yield curve:

    +50 bp   82.51
    −50 bp   88.63

    This bond's effective duration is *closest* to:

    A. 3.6.
    B. 6.0.
    C. 7.2.

© Kaplan, Inc.

−1

Additional Problems

2) For the owner of a 20-year 5% BBB-rated bond, an increase in yield-to-maturity just shortly after the bond is purchased will:

A. increase the bondholder's yield if her holding period is relatively short.

B. increase the bondholder's yield if she holds the bond until maturity.

C. decrease the bondholder's yield regardless of her investment horizon.

- 1

CFA Curriculum Vol. 5,
R.55, Q.18, p. 577

4) A bond with exactly nine years remaining until maturity offers a 3% coupon rate with annual coupons. The bond, with a yield-to-maturity of 5%, is priced at 85.784357 per 100 of par value. The estimated price value of a basis point for the bond is *closest* to:

A. 0.0086.

B. 0.0648.

C. 0.1295.

- 2

CFA Curriculum Vol. 5,
R.55, Q.20, p. 578

3) A bond is currently trading for 98.722 per 100 of par value. If the bond's yield-to-maturity (YTM) rises by 10 basis points, the bond's full price is expected to fall to 98.669. If the bond's YTM decreases by 10 basis points, the bond's full price is expected to increase to 98.782. The bond's approximate convexity is *closest* to:

A. 0.071.

B. 70.906.

C. 1,144,628.

- 1

Additional Problems

5) A 6-year, 7% coupon, option-free bond has an effective duration of 4 and an effective convexity of 11.79. If interest rates increase by 25 basis points across the entire yield curve, the price of the bond will *most likely*:

A. decrease by more than 1%.

B. decrease by less than 1%.

C. increase by less than 1%.

- 2

Additional Problems

6) A bond has an embedded option, either a put or a call. The bond has an OAS that is greater than its Z-spread. It is *most likely* that the bond, compared to an otherwise identical option-free bond, will have:

A. negative convexity at relatively low yields.
B. lower interest rate risk at relatively high yields.
C. greater duration at relatively low yields.

STUDY SESSION 16 ANSWERS

Reading	Slide Number	Answer
55	3	C
55	5	C
55	7	B
55	13	C
55	18	A
55	30	C
56	39	A

Additional Problems

1. C

2. B

3. B

4. B

5. B

6. B

Study Session 17

Derivatives

Derivatives

Derivatives

Derivatives

57. Derivative Markets and Instruments

KAPLAN | SCHOOL OF PROFESSIONAL
UNIVERSITY | AND CONTINUING EDUCATION | SCHWESER

Derivatives

Study Session 17
Derivatives

57. Derivative Markets and Instruments
58. Basics of Derivative Pricing and Valuation
59. Risk Management Applications of Option
   Strategies

KAPLAN | SCHOOL OF PROFESSIONAL
UNIVERSITY | AND CONTINUING EDUCATION | SCHWESER

© Kaplan, Inc.

Derivative Markets and Instruments

LOS 57.b Contrast
CFAI p. 7, Schweser p. 151

Forward Commitments and
Contingent Claims

Futures, forward contracts, and **swaps** are forward commitments

Options and **credit derivatives** are contingent claims because one party's obligation depends on an event

- Credit derivatives: Borrower credit event
- Options: Exercise by holder

  <u>Call</u>: Right to buy   <u>Put</u>: Right to sell

© Kaplan, Inc.

3

Derivative Markets and Instruments

LOS 57.a Define/Distinguish
CFAI p. 6, Schweser p. 151

Derivatives

A **derivative security** derives its value from the price of another (underlying) asset or an interest rate

Futures and some options are traded on organized exchanges

Forward contracts, swaps, credit derivatives, and **some options** are custom instruments created by dealers

© Kaplan, Inc.

2

Forward Contract Example

The **long** agrees to buy 100 oz. of gold on Aug 15 for $1,200/oz.

The **short** agrees to sell 100 oz. of gold on Aug 15 for $1,200/oz.

Neither pays to enter the contract.

On Aug 15, if:

- Spot gold is *above* $1,200, long has gains
- Spot gold is *below* $1,200, short has gains
- Spot gold is at $1,238, long gains $3,800

© Kaplan, Inc.

4

Forward Contracts

- Customized: No active secondary market
- Long obligated to buy; short obligated to sell
- Specified asset (currency, stock, index, bond)
- Specified date in the future
- Long gains if asset price above forward price
- Short gains if asset price below forward price
- Deliverable or cash-settled

© Kaplan, Inc.

5

Futures Contracts

- Like forward contracts but **standardized**
- **Exchange-traded**, active secondary market
- **Require margin** deposit, mark to market, daily settlement based on settle price
- **Deposit required** if margin < maintenance margin
- **No default** (counterparty) risk
- Limits on daily price moves, locked limit

© Kaplan, Inc.

6

Swaps

- Equivalent to a series of forward contracts
- Simple interest rate swap
  - One party pays a fixed rate of interest
  - One party pays a variable (floating) rate of interest
- Payments can be based on interest rates or stock/portfolio/index returns
- Can involve two different currencies

© Kaplan, Inc.

7

LOS 57.c Define/Compare
CFAI p. 14, Schweser p. 152

Swap Example

Banco Lindo agrees to pay 6-month Libor for the prior period times $10 million, every six months for two years.

Banco Rio agrees to pay 5% × 10 million × ½ = $250,000 every six months, for two years.

If 6-month Libor is 4%, at the end of six months Banco Lindo will owe 4% × 10 million × ½ = $200,000.

The payments are netted, Banco Rio will pay Banco Lindo the difference of $50,000.

© Kaplan, Inc.

8

LOS 57.c Define/Compare
CFAI p. 14, Schweser p. 152

Credit Derivatives

Credit default swap: Lender pays periodic cash flows to protection seller, receives payment if credit event occurs—similar to insurance contract

Total return swap: One party pays fixed or floating rate of interest, the other pays the total return (interest plus price change) on a risky credit

Credit spread option: Option for which the underlying is the credit spread on a bond

© Kaplan, Inc.

9

LOS 57.d Describe
CFAI p. 39, Schweser p. 157

Benefits of Derivatives

- Provide price information, estimate the price of uncertainty and the volatility of asset returns

- High liquidity

- Lower transactions costs, easier to go short

- Allow the transfer of risk and management of risk

- Improve market efficiency of market prices

© Kaplan, Inc.

10

LOS 57.e Explain
CFAI p. 47, Schweser p. 157

Role of Arbitrage

Arbitrage is possible when two securities or portfolios have **identical future payoffs** but **different market prices.**

Trading by arbitrageurs will continue until they affect supply and demand enough to bring asset prices to efficient (no-arbitrage) levels.

Arbitrage relations (law of one price) are used to value derivatives.

© Kaplan, Inc.

11

Exchange-traded derivatives are:

A. largely unregulated.

B. traded through an informal network.

C. guaranteed by a clearinghouse against default.

12 – 1

The derivative that is *least likely* a contingent claim
is a(n):

A. put option.

B. equity swap.

C. credit default swap.

© Kaplan, Inc.

13 – 1

Derivatives

58. Basics of Derivative
Pricing and Valuation

Asset Values

General form of asset valuation:

$$S_0 = E(S_T) / (1 + Rf + RP)$$

$E(S_T)$ Expected asset price at time T

Rf   Opportunity cost

RP   Risk premium for uncertainty about S_T

Risk premium depends on investor risk aversion

© Kaplan, Inc.

15

Basics of Derivative Pricing and Valuation

LOS 58.a Explain
CFAI p. 66, Schweser p. 162

Derivatives Values

Derivatives pricing is based on a **No-arbitrage condition—Law of one price**

Risky bond + Total return swap = Risk-free bond

Risky asset – Forward = Risk-free asset

– Asset + Forward = Risk-free asset

Risk-free bond + Forward = Risky Asset

© Kaplan, Inc.

16

Basics of Derivative Pricing and Valuation

LOS 58.a Explain
CFAI p. 66, Schweser p. 162

Limitations on Arbitrage

- Assets may be difficult to sell short

- Transactions costs

- Lack of accurate information (e.g., option volatility)

- Arbitrage may not be risk free

© Kaplan, Inc.

17

Basics of Derivative Pricing and Valuation

LOS 58.b Distinguish
CFAI p. 72, Schweser p. 165

Forwards and Futures: Value vs. Price

Forward at time 0: promise to buy asset at time T

Price = $F_0(T)$, forward price in contract

Value = Value of a long position in the forward

Value is zero at initiation (time 0) if....

© Kaplan, Inc.

18

Basics of Derivative Pricing and Valuation

LOS 58.c Explain
CFAI p. 73, Schweser p. 166

No-Arbitrage Forward Price

$F_0(T) = S_0(1 + Rf)^T$ or $F_0(T)/S_0 = (1 + Rf)^T$

If forward price is "too high":
Short forward, borrow at Rf, buy the asset

If forward price is "too low":
Short asset, invest at Rf, long forward

© Kaplan, Inc.

19

Forward Contract Value

Value of forward at time t (during contract life):

$$V_t(T) = S_t - F_0(T)/(1 + Rf)^{(T-t)}$$

Value of forward at expiration (settlement):

$$V_T(T) = S_T - F_0(T)$$

Forward Value with Benefits and Costs

Value of forward **at initiation of the contract**

$$V_0(T) = S_0 - PV_0(Ben) + PV_0(Cost) - F_0(T)/(1 + Rf)^T$$

$\underbrace{\hspace{3cm}}_{\text{Net cost of carry}}$

S_0	Asset price at time t
Rf	Opportunity cost of funds
$PV_0(Cost)$	Storage, insurance initiation to T
$PV_0(Ben)$	Cash flows (monetary benefits)
	+ convenience yield (nonmonetary benefits) initiation to T

Forward Value at Time = t

Value of forward **at time t** w/costs and benefits

$$V_t(T) = S_t - PV_t(Ben) + PV_t(Cost) - F_0(T)/(1 + Rf)^{(T-t)}$$

$\underbrace{\hspace{3cm}}_{\text{Net cost of carry}}$

S_t	Asset price at time t
Rf	Opportunity cost of funds
$PV_t(Cost)$	Storage, insurance from t to T
$PV_t(Ben)$	Cash flows (monetary benefits)
	+ convenience yield (nonmonetary benefits) from t to T

If the present value of storage costs exceeds the present value of its convenience yield, then the commodity's forward price is *most likely*:

A. less than the spot price compounded at the risk-free rate.

B. the same as the spot price compounded at the risk-free rate.

C. higher than the spot price compounded at the risk-free rate.

LOS 58.e Define/Describe
CFAI p. 77, Schweser p. 167
**Basics of Derivative
Pricing and Valuation**

Forward Rate Agreement (FRA)

Exchange fixed-rate for floating-rate payment

- Notional amount
- Fixed rate = forward (contract) rate
- Floating rate (e.g., Libor) is underlying rate
- Long pays fixed rate, receives Libor
  Receives [Libor – fixed rate] **or**
  Pays [fixed rate – Libor]

© Kaplan, Inc.

24

LOS 58.e Define/Describe
CFAI p. 77, Schweser p. 167
**Basics of Derivative
Pricing and Valuation**

Forward Rate Agreement (FRA)

Borrow for 90 days,
starting 30 days from now

0   30   60   90   120

Synthetic FRA

Borrow for 120 days

0   30   60   90   120

Lend for 30 days

© Kaplan, Inc.

25

LOS 58.f Explain
CFAI p. 80, Schweser p. 169
**Basics of Derivative
Pricing and Valuation**

Forward Prices vs. Futures Prices

- Unlike forwards, futures contracts are **marked to market** daily, so futures have interim cash flows
- Value of futures = gain/loss since previous day; resets to zero daily at settlement
- Futures prices = forward prices if interest rates are constant or not correlated with futures prices
- If interest rates are positively correlated with futures prices long futures are more desirable
- Essentially no difference for valuation

© Kaplan, Inc.

26

LOS 58.g,h Explain/Distinguish
CFAI p. 82, Schweser p. 170
**Basics of Derivative
Pricing and Valuation**

Interest Rate Swaps

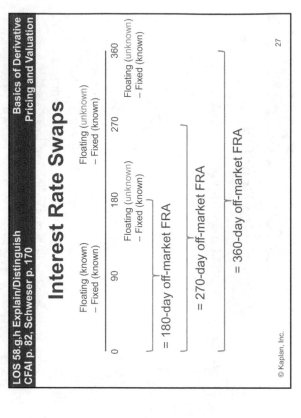

Floating (known)
– Fixed (known)

Floating (unknown)
– Fixed (known)

0   90   180   270   360

Floating (unknown)
– Fixed (known)

Floating (unknown)
– Fixed (known)

= 180-day off-market FRA

= 270-day off-market FRA

= 360-day off-market FRA

© Kaplan, Inc.

27

Interest Rate Swaps

- To replicate a swap with zero value at initiation, present values of off-market FRAs must sum to zero

- Swap price is the fixed rate

- Swap value is positive if expected short-term rates increase, negative if expected short-term rates decrease

28

European Options

Exercise value of European **call** = Max$\{0, (S_T - X)\}$

   Call is in the money if $S_T > X$

   Out of the money if $S_T < X$

Exercise value of European **put** = Max$\{0, (X - S_T)\}$

   Put is in the money if $S_T < X$

   Put is out of the money if $S_T > X$

Intrinsic or exercise value is amount in the money

Option price = intrinsic value + time value

29

Factors That Affect Option Values

European options

- Asset price
- Exercise price
- Volatility of asset price
- Time to expiration
- Risk-free rate
- Cash flows from and costs of holding assets

30

Factors That Affect Option Values

Higher asset price: *increases* call values
                                 decreases put values

Higher exercise price: *decreases* call values
                                 increases put values

Higher volatility: *increases both* call
                                 and put values

31

Factors That Affect Option Values

Longer time to expiration: *increases both call and put values*

> *Except for European style puts under some conditions (long time to expiration, high Rf, deep in the money)*

Higher Rf: *increases call values*
decreases put values

32

Factors That Affect Option Values

Cash flows to underlying: *decrease call values*
increase put values

Carrying costs: *increase call values*
decrease put values

33

If the risk-free rate increases, the value of an in-the-money European put option will *most likely*:

A. decrease.

B. remain the same.

C. increase.

34 - 1

Deriving Put-Call Parity (European Options)

Protective put = stock + put

If $S \leq X$, payoff = $S + (X - S) = X$
If $S \geq X$, payoff = $S + 0 = S$

Fiduciary call = call + $X / (1 + RFR)^T$
(bond that pays X at maturity)

If $S \leq X$, payoff = $0 + X = X$
If $S \geq X$, payoff = $(S - X) + X = S$

Same payoffs means same values by no-arbitrage
Put-call parity: $S + P = C + X / (1 + RFR)^T$

35

Parity Conditions and Synthetic Options

$$S + P = C + \frac{X}{(1+RFR)^T} \quad \text{can be rearranged}$$

$$\text{to get } P = C - S + \frac{X}{(1+RFR)^T}$$

$$\text{and } C = P + S - \frac{X}{(1+RFR)^T}$$

36

Put-Call-Forward Parity

We can replicate the underlying asset with a forward contract and a risk-free bond that pays the forward price at expiration: $\quad S_0 = F_0(T)/(1 + RFR)^T$

<u>Same relationships hold:</u>

Put-call parity: $S + P = C + X / (1 + RFR)^T$

Put-call forward parity:

$F_0(T)/(1 + RFR)^T + P = C + X / (1 + RFR)^T$

37

Binomial Model for Option Pricing

Next period, asset price will change to one of two possible values

U = size of up-move = 1.15

D = size of down-move = $\frac{1}{U}$ = 0.87

π_u = risk-neutral probability of up-move = $\frac{1 + R_f - D}{U - D}$ = 0.715

π_D = risk-neutral probability of down-move = $1 - \pi_u$ = 0.285

R_f = 7%; S_0 = $30

38

Binomial Model: Example

One-period binomial tree for stock price

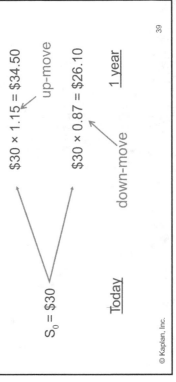

39

Binomial Model

$rnp_U = 0.715$

$S_0 = \$30$

$rnp_D = 0.285$

$S = \$30 \times 1.15 = \$34.50$
$C = max (0, \$34.50 - \$30) = \$4.50$

$S = \$30 \times 0.87 = \$26.10$
$C = max (0, \$26.10 - \$30) = \$0$

Today   1 year

© Kaplan, Inc.

41

European vs. American Option Value

American options can be exercised early

Early exercise of call options is valuable if the asset pays interest or dividends

Early exercise of put options can be valuable if they are deep in the money

© Kaplan, Inc.

43

Binomial Model

With an up-move:
- Stock increases to $34.50
- Payoff to call with $30 exercise = $4.50

With a down move:
- Stock falls to $26.10
- Option will pay $0 (option out-of-the-money)

© Kaplan, Inc.

40

The Binomial Model

Call value = PV of cash flows (discounted at R_f):

$$C_0 = \frac{(\$4.50 \times 0.715) + (\$0 \times 0.285)}{1.07}$$

$$= \frac{\$3.22}{1.07} = \$3.01$$

© Kaplan, Inc.

42

Derivatives

Derivatives

59. Risk Management Applications of Option Strategies

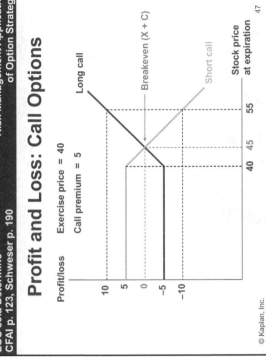

KAPLAN UNIVERSITY SCHOOL OF PROFESSIONAL AND CONTINUING EDUCATION | SCHWESER

A synthetic put option can be created with a portfolio consisting of:

A. a long call position, a short asset position, and a long bond position.

B. a long asset position, short bond position, and a short call position.

C. a long bond position, a short call position, and a short asset position.

44 - 1

© Kaplan, Inc.

Profit and Loss: Call Options

Exercise price = 40

Call premium = 5

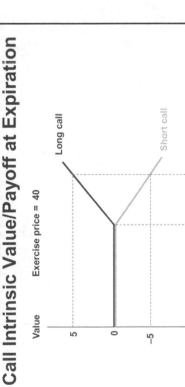

© Kaplan, Inc.

47

Call Intrinsic Value/Payoff at Expiration

Exercise price = 40

© Kaplan, Inc.

46

LOS 59.a Determine
CFAI p. 123, Schweser p. 190

Put Intrinsic Value/Payoff at Expiration

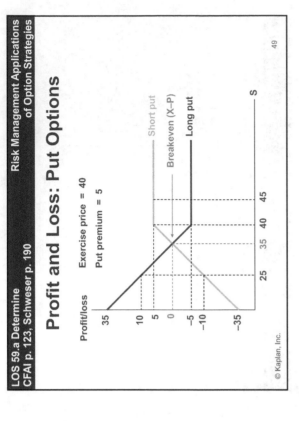

Exercise price = 40

© Kaplan, Inc.   48

LOS 59.a Determine
CFAI p. 123, Schweser p. 190

Profit and Loss: Put Options

Exercise price = 40

Put premium = 5

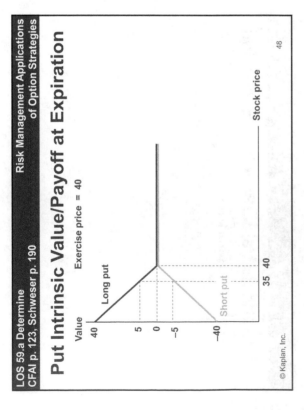

© Kaplan, Inc.   49

Consider a 40 call purchased at $3.00 when the stock is trading at $39.00

1. **Maximum profit:**
2. **Maximum loss:**
3. **Breakeven:**
4. **Option value and gain or loss if stock price is $42.00 at expiration:**

© Kaplan, Inc.   50 - 4

LOS 59.b Determine/Explain
CFAI p. 130, Schweser p. 194

Covered Call Strategy (Position)

- Writer owns the stock and sells a call
- Any loss will be reduced by premium received
- Writer trades the stock's upside potential for the option premium

© Kaplan, Inc.   51

Slide 52-6

For a position consisting of a stock bought at $39 and a call option at 40 that was sold for $3, calculate the following:

1. **Net cost of position**:
2. **Breakeven stock price at expiration**:
3. **Maximum gain**:
4. **Maximum loss**:
5. **Profit/loss at stock price of 39**:
6. **Profit/loss at stock price of 32**:

52 - 6

Slide 53

Payoff and Profits: Covered Call

Exercise price = 40
Call premium = 3
Net cost = 39 − 3 = 36
Breakeven = 36

53

Slide 54

Protective Put Strategy (Position)

- Long the stock and long a put
- Any gain on the stock will be reduced by premium paid for the put
- Put buyer pays for protection against stock price falling below the strike price

54

Slide 55-6

An investor buys a stock at $41 and buys a 40 put for $3. Calculate the:

1. **Cost** of the position =
2. **Breakeven** stock price at expiration =
3. **Maximum gain**:
4. **Maximum loss**:

5. At stock price of 47 → profit =
6. At stock price of 38 → loss =

55 - 6

Derivatives

Additional Problems

Additional Problems

2) Tony Mart notes that the Federal Reserve has begun to decrease the rate of growth of the money supply. Which of the following reflects the *most likely* effect of this change in monetary policy on the value of Zeta Corp. put and call options?

	Put	Call
A.	Increase	Decrease
B.	Decrease	Increase
C.	Decrease	Decrease

-1

LOS 59.b Determine/Explain   Risk Management Applications
CFAI p. 130, Schweser p. 194   of Option Strategies

Payoff and Profit: **Protective Put**

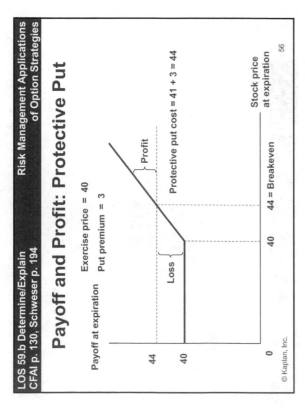

Exercise price = 40
Put premium = 3

Payoff at expiration

Profit

Protective put cost = 41 + 3 = 44

44

40

Loss

0   40

44 = Breakeven

Stock price at expiration

56

Additional Problems

1) 9-month 45 puts and 45 calls on Astro stock are trading at $1.25 and $6.75. Astro does not pay dividends and is trading at $47/share. If the risk-free rate is 4%, which portfolio would produce an arbitrage profit?

A. Long the call and a bond, short the stock and put.

B. Borrow funds, short the put and call, long the stock.

C. Borrow funds, short the call, long the stock and put.

-4

Additional Problems

4) An asset priced at S_0 has a positive convenience yield and no storage costs or cash flows. The price of a 1-year forward contract on this asset, at initiation, is:

   A. zero, regardless of the asset price.

   B. greater than $S_0(1 + Rf)$.

   C. less than $S_0(1 + Rf)$.

- 1

CFA Curriculum Vol. 6, R.58, Q.32, p. 112

3) Which of the following is *least likely* to be required by the binomial option pricing model?

   A. Spot price.

   B. Two possible prices one period later.

   C. Actual probabilities of the up and down moves.

- 1

STUDY SESSION 17 ANSWERS

Reading	Slide Number	Answer
57	12	C
57	13	B
58	23	C
58	34	A
58	44	A
59	50(1)	Unlimited
59	50(2)	$3
59	50(3)	$43
59	50(4)	Value = $2, loss = $1
59	52(1)	$36
59	52(2)	$36
59	52(3)	$4
59	52(4)	$36
59	52(5)	$3
59	52(6)	–$4
59	55(1)	$44
59	55(2)	$44
59	55(3)	Unlimited
59	55(4)	$4
59	55(5)	$3
59	55(6)	$4

Additional Problems

1. C

2. B

3. C

4. C

Study Session 18

Alternative Investments

Study Session 18
Alternative Investments

60. Introduction to Alternative Investments

KAPLAN UNIVERSITY | SCHOOL OF PROFESSIONAL AND CONTINUING EDUCATION | SCHWESER

Alternative Investments

60. Introduction to Alternative Investments

KAPLAN UNIVERSITY | SCHOOL OF PROFESSIONAL AND CONTINUING EDUCATION | SCHWESER

LOS 60.a Compare
CFAI p. 150, Schweser p. 201

Alternative vs. Traditional Investments

- Different types of assets held, structure of investment vehicles
- Higher fees (management, incentive)
- Less liquid
- Less regulated, less transparent
- Different tax treatments

2

LOS 60.b Describe
CFAI p. 154, Schweser p. 201

Categories of Alternative Investments

- Hedge funds
- Private equity
- Real estate
- Commodities
- Infrastructure
- Others (e.g., collectibles, patents)

3

Benefits of Alternative Investments

Potential portfolio diversification benefits

- Low correlation with traditional investment returns

- Higher average returns than traditional investments

However, return measures are biased upward, risk measures are biased downward

- Survivorship bias

- Backfill bias

© Kaplan, Inc.

4

Hedge Funds

- Structured as limited partnerships

- Use leverage, derivatives, short selling

- Limited to qualified investors

Lockup period: Minimum time before investor can withdraw funds

Notice period: Days within which a fund must fulfill a redemption request

© Kaplan, Inc.

5

Hedge Fund Strategies

1. Event-driven strategies

Merger arbitrage: Buy shares of firm being acquired, short shares of acquirer

Distressed/restructuring: Buy if restructuring will increase value

Activist shareholder: Gain board seats to influence company decisions

Special situations: Spinoffs, asset sales, security issuance or repurchase

© Kaplan, Inc.

6

Hedge Fund Strategies

2. Relative value strategies

Convertible arbitrage: Convertible bonds versus underlying common stock

Asset-backed: ABS, MBS

General fixed income

Volatility: Trade options based on implied versus expected volatility

Multi-strategy: Across asset classes

© Kaplan, Inc.

7

Hedge Fund Strategies

3. Macro strategies: Trade securities, currencies, commodities based on global economic trends

4. Equity hedge fund strategies

Market neutral: Equal values in long and short positions

Fundamental growth: Identify high-growth companies

© Kaplan, Inc.

8

Hedge Fund Strategies (continued)

4. Equity hedge fund strategies (continued)

Fundamental value: Identify undervalued companies

Quantitative directional: May have net long or short exposure

Short bias: Net short exposure

Fund of funds: Invest in multiple hedge funds

© Kaplan, Inc.

9

A hedge fund manager has taken a large leveraged position long the euro and an equally large leveraged position short the yen. The *most likely* classification of this hedge fund strategy is:

A.   market neutral.

B.   special situations.

C.   macro strategy.

© Kaplan, Inc.

10 - 1

Private Equity

Firms that invest in private companies or take public companies private

Private equity strategies:

- Leveraged buyout ⎤
- Venture capital   ⎦ Focus for exam
- Developmental capital / minority equity / private investment in public equity (PIPE)
- Distressed investing

© Kaplan, Inc.

11

Leveraged Buyouts

Most common private equity strategy

Funded by debt

Bank debt, high yield bonds

Mezzanine financing: Subordinated debt, includes warrants or conversion to equity

Management buyout: Current managers involved in purchase, remain with company

Management buy-in: Replace managers of acquired company

© Kaplan, Inc.

12

Venture Capital

1. Formative stage

Angel investing: Business plans, market potential

Seed stage: Product development, market research

Early stage: Begin production and sales

2. Later stage: Company expansion

3. Mezzanine stage: Prepare for IPO

© Kaplan, Inc.

13

Private Equity Structure and Fees

- Typically structured as limited partnership
- Investors provide **committed capital** which fund managers draw down to invest in portfolio companies
  - Management fees typically 1% to 3% of committed capital
  - Incentive fees typically 20% of profits

    Fees paid periodically may exceed 20% of profits over time: Clawback provision requires managers to return excess fees

© Kaplan, Inc.

14

Private Equity Exit Strategies

Trade sale: Sell portfolio company to competitor

Secondary sale: Sell portfolio company to other private equity investors

IPO: Sell portfolio company shares to public

Recapitalization: Issue portfolio company debt to fund dividend payment (to private equity owner)

Write-off/liquidation: Take loss

© Kaplan, Inc.

15

Real Estate

Residential property

Commercial property

Mortgages, mortgage-backed securities

Real Estate Investment Trusts (REITs)

Farmland, timberland

Commodities

Commodities exposure most commonly gained through derivatives rather than outright ownership

Return comes from price changes (no income)

Hedge inflation risk

Commodities

Commodity ETFs: Available to investors who are restricted to equity shares

Shares of commodity producers: Less-than-perfect correlation with commodity prices

Managed futures funds: Active management of commodity investments

Individual (separately) managed accounts

Commodity sector funds (e.g., energy, metals)

Infrastructure

Long-lived assets that provide public services

Economic infrastructure
- Transportation (e.g., roads, bridges, airports)
- Utility assets (e.g., pipelines, communications)

Social infrastructure (e.g., schools, hospitals, prisons)

Brownfield investments (existing infrastructure) have more stable earnings, higher payout ratios, but less growth potential, compared to **greenfield investments** (infrastructure to be built)

LOS 60.d Describe
CFAI p. 158, Schweser p. 203

Introduction to
Alternative Investments

Infrastructure

Direct investment: Large size, very low liquidity, must operate and maintain physical assets

Indirect investment vehicles:
- Publicly-traded infrastructure securities
- Master limited partnerships
- Shares of firms
- Exchange-traded funds
- Listed mutual funds
- Private equity funds
- Unlisted mutual funds

© Kaplan, Inc.

20

LOS 60.e Describe/Calculate/Interpret
CFAI p. 166, Schweser p. 213

Introduction to
Alternative Investments

Hedge Fund Fees

- *2 and 20:* 2% management fee, 20% incentive fee
- Management fee may be calculated on beginning or ending assets
- Incentive fee may be
- **net** of (after) management fees or **independent** of management fees
- **Fund of funds** typically charges *1 and 10* in addition to fees paid to underlying hedge funds

© Kaplan, Inc.

21

LOS 60.e Describe/Calculate/Interpret
CFAI p. 166, Schweser p. 213

Introduction to
Alternative Investments

Hedge Fund Fees

Hard hurdle rate: Incentive fees only on gains above hurdle rate

Soft hurdle rate: Incentive fees on all gains, but only if return exceeds hurdle rate

High water mark: Incentive fees only on gains that increase assets above highest previous value

© Kaplan, Inc.

22

LOS 60.e Describe/Calculate/Interpret
CFAI p. 166, Schweser p. 213

Introduction to
Alternative Investments

Hedge Fund Fees

Asset values (before fees) are $110.0 million at initiation, $102.2 million at the end of Year 1, and $118.0 million at the end of Year 2.

Fee structure:
- 2 and 20 based on beginning assets
- Incentive fees net of management fees
- Soft hurdle rate of 5%
- High water mark

Calculate the net return for Year 1 and Year 2

© Kaplan, Inc.

23

Hedge Fund Fees Example

Year 2

- Beginning value net of fees = $102.2 – $2.2 = $100.0 million

- Management fee = $100.0 × 0.02 = $2.0 million

- Return net of management fee = [($118.0 – $2.0) / $100] – 1 = 16.0%

- Incentive fee = ($118.0 – $2.0 – $110.0) × 0.20 = $1.2 million
  High water mark

- Net return to investors = [($118.0 – $2.0 – $1.2) / $100.0] – 1 = 14.8%

© Kaplan, Inc.

25 - 5

Private Equity Valuation

Same techniques used to value publicly traded companies are used to value private equity portfolio companies

- Market/comparables approach
- Discounted cash flow approach
- Asset-based approach

Private companies may require different discount rates or price multiples than publicly traded companies

© Kaplan, Inc.

27

Hedge Fund Fees Example

Year 1

- Management fee = $110.0 million × 0.02 = $2.2 million

- Return net of management fee = [($102.2 – $2.2) / $110.0] – 1 = –9.1%

- No incentive fee: Return < hurdle rate

- Total fees = $2.2 million

© Kaplan, Inc.

24 - 4

Hedge Fund Valuation Issues

- Should use bid prices for long positions, ask prices for short positions

- Values of non-traded securities estimated with pricing models

- Illiquid securities
  ➢ Reduce market price to account for illiquidity based on size of position held
  ➢ Trading NAV is adjusted (downward) for illiquidity

© Kaplan, Inc.

26

Real Estate Valuation

Comparable sales approach: Recent sales of similar properties

Income approach
- Present value of future cash flows from property
- Net operating income / capitalization rate

Cost approach: Replacement cost, including land and current costs to rebuild

© Kaplan, Inc.   28

Real Estate Investment Trust Valuation

Income based: Similar to direct capitalization
- Funds from operations (FFO)
- Adjusted funds from operations (AFFO)
- Capitalization rates

Asset-based:

$$NAV = \frac{\text{market value of assets} - \text{market value of liabilities}}{\text{number of REIT shares outstanding}}$$

© Kaplan, Inc.   29

Commodities Valuation

Futures price ≈ spot price × (1 + risk-free rate)
+ storage costs
− convenience yield

Convenience yield: Value of having physical commodity available for use

Low convenience yield → **contango**
Futures price > spot price

High convenience yield → **backwardation**
Spot price > futures price

© Kaplan, Inc.   30

Risk Management of Alternative Investments

Standard deviation is not the most appropriate risk measure

- Fat tails, negative skewness
- Returns smoothed by use of model values or use of appraised asset values
- Use measures of downside risk (e.g., value-at-risk or Sortino ratio)

© Kaplan, Inc.   31

Risk Management of Alternative Investments

LOS 60.g Describe
CFAI p. 202, Schweser p. 218

- Risks from use of derivatives (counterparty, liquidity, operational, financial)

- Performance depends on managers' skill

- Lack of transparency

- Illiquidity

- Correlations with traditional investment returns vary over time, *may increase during crisis periods*

© Kaplan, Inc.

32

Effects of survivorship bias and backfill bias in alternative investment data on the risk and return statistics for this asset class will be:

	Risk	Return
A.	overstated	overstated
B.	overstated	understated
C.	understated	overstated

© Kaplan, Inc.

33 - 2

Alternative Investments

Additional Problems

KAPLAN UNIVERSITY   SCHOOL OF PROFESSIONAL AND CONTINUING EDUCATION | SCHWESER

Additional Problems

1) A hedge fund has a "2 and 20" fee structure, incentive fees are independent of management fees, and a hard hurdle rate of 3%. If the gross fund return is 15%, what is the investor's net return?

A. 10.0%.
B. 10.4%.
C. 10.6%.

© Kaplan, Inc.

- 1

CFA Curriculum Vol. 6,
R.60, Q.5, p. 210

2) An investor is *most likely* to consider adding alternative investments to a traditional investment portfolio because:

A. of their historically higher returns.

B. of their historically low standard deviation of returns.

C. their inclusion is expected to reduce the portfolio's Sharpe ratio.

- 5

CFA Curriculum Vol. 6,
R.60, Q.11, p. 211

3) If a commodity's forward curve is in contango, the component of a commodities futures return *most likely* to reflect this is:

A. the spot price.

B. the roll yield.

C. the collateral yield.

- 2

STUDY SESSION 18 ANSWERS

Reading	Slide Number	Answer
60	10	C
60	33	C

Additional Problems

1. C

2. A

3. B

Appendix

Ethical and Professional Standards

Ethical and Professional Standards

Ethics and Trust in the Investment Profession

KAPLAN
UNIVERSITY   SCHOOL OF PROFESSIONAL
AND CONTINUING EDUCATION | SCHWESER

LOS a Describe   Ethics and Trust in the Investment Profession

Ethics

- A set of shared beliefs about good (acceptable) or bad (unacceptable) behavior

- Study of good and bad behavior

In investment profession:
Conduct that balances self-interest and impact on outcomes for *stakeholders*

© Kaplan, Inc.

2

LOS b Describe   Ethics and Trust in the Investment Profession

Role of a Code of Ethics

To communicate to the public that a profession's members will use their knowledge and skills to serve their clients in an honest and ethical manner

© Kaplan, Inc.

3

LOS c Identify   Ethics and Trust in the Investment Profession

Challenges to Ethical Behavior

Individuals overrate the ethical quality of their behavior

Importance of situational (external) influences:

- Social pressure
- Loyalty to employer, supervisor, or co-worker
- Money, power, or prestige

© Kaplan, Inc.

4

LOS e Distinguish   Ethics and Trust in the Investment Profession

Ethical and Legal Standards

Some actions may be <u>illegal but ethical</u>
Example: Civil disobedience

Some actions may be <u>legal but unethical</u>
Example: Taking shares in oversubscribed IPO instead of allocating them to clients

In general, ethical principles set a higher standard than laws and regulations

© Kaplan, Inc.   6

LOS d Describe   Ethics and Trust in the Investment Profession

Need for High Ethical Standards in the Investment Industry

A lack of trust in investment professionals:

- Makes potential investors less likely to use investment industry services
- Increases perceived risk of providing capital; increases the cost of capital

Providing incomplete or false information leads to misallocation of capital and slower growth

© Kaplan, Inc.   5 - 3

LOS f Describe/Apply   Ethics and Trust in the Investment Profession

Framework for Ethical Decision Making

1. Identify facts available or needed; ethical principles; stakeholders and conflicts
2. Consider alternatives and situational influences; seek guidance
3. Make a decision and act on it
4. Evaluate outcome: Intended results? Ethical principles considered adequately?

© Kaplan, Inc.   7 - 4

Ethics and Standards

Ethical and Professional Standards

Code of Ethics and Standards of Professional Conduct

KAPLAN UNIVERSITY | SCHOOL OF PROFESSIONAL AND CONTINUING EDUCATION | **SCHWESER**

Code and Standards

CFA Institute Professional Conduct Program

Disciplinary Review Committee of CFA Institute Board of Governors has responsibility for the Professional Conduct Program and for enforcement of the Code and Standards

CFA Institute, through Professional Conduct staff, conducts **inquiries related to professional conduct**

© Kaplan, Inc.

2

Code and Standards

CFA Institute Professional Conduct Program

Inquiry can be prompted by:

- **Self-disclosure** by members or candidates
- **Written complaints** about a member or candidate's professional conduct
- **Evidence of misconduct** by a member or candidate

© Kaplan, Inc.

3

Code and Standards

CFA Institute Professional Conduct Program

Inquiry can be prompted by:

- Report by a **CFA exam proctor**
- **Analysis** of exam scores and materials, **monitoring** of websites and social media

© Kaplan, Inc.

4

Code and Standards

CFA Institute Professional Conduct Program

CFA Institute Professional Conduct staff may decide:

1. That no disciplinary sanctions are appropriate
2. To issue a cautionary letter
3. To discipline the member or candidate

Sanctions may include condemnation by member's peers or suspension of candidate's participation in the CFA Program

© Kaplan, Inc.

5

Code and Standards

Code of Ethics

Act with integrity, competence, diligence, respect, and in an ethical manner—public, clients, prospects, employers, employees, colleagues. *Act in an ethical manner.*

Integrity of investment profession and client interests above personal interests. *Integrity is paramount and clients always come first.*

© Kaplan, Inc.

6

Code and Standards

Code of Ethics

Reasonable care, independent professional judgment when conducting analysis, making recommendations, taking investment actions, and in other professional activities. *Use reasonable care; be independent.*

Practice, encourage others...in a professional, ethical manner...reflect credit on themselves and profession. *Be a credit to the investment profession.*

© Kaplan, Inc.

7

Code and Standards

Code of Ethics

Promote integrity of capital markets for ultimate benefit of society. *Uphold capital market rules and regulations.*

Maintain, improve professional competence, and strive to do the same for other investment professionals. *Be competent.*

© Kaplan, Inc.

8

Standards of Professional Conduct
I. Professionalism
- A. Knowledge of the Law
- B. Independence and Objectivity
- C. Misrepresentation
- D. Misconduct

© Kaplan, Inc.

9

Standards of Professional Conduct
II. Integrity of Capital Markets
- A. Material Nonpublic Information
- B. Market Manipulation

© Kaplan, Inc.

10

Standards of Professional Conduct
III. Duties to Clients
- A. Loyalty, Prudence, and Care
- B. Fair Dealing
- C. Suitability
- D. Performance Presentation
- E. Preservation of Confidentiality

© Kaplan, Inc.

11

Standards of Professional Conduct
IV. Duties to Employers
- A. Loyalty
- B. Additional Compensation Arrangements
- C. Responsibilities of Supervisors

© Kaplan, Inc.

12

Standards of Professional Conduct

V. Investment Analysis, Recommendations, and Actions

A. Diligence and Reasonable Basis

B. Communication with Clients and Prospective Clients

C. Record Retention

Standards of Professional Conduct

VI. Conflicts of Interest

A. Disclosure of Conflicts

B. Priority of Transactions

C. Referral Fees

Standards of Professional Conduct

VII. Responsibilities as a CFA Institute Member or CFA Candidate

A. Conduct as Participants in CFA Institute Programs

B. Reference to CFA Institute, the CFA Designation, and the CFA Program

Standard I:
Professionalism

Ethical and Professional Standards

Guidance for Standards I - VII

Standard I: Professionalism

Standard I(A) - Knowledge of the Law
Guidance

- Most strict
- First, notify supervisor or compliance
- May confront wrongdoer directly
- Dissociate if necessary
- Inaction may be construed as participation
- No requirement to report violations to governmental authorities, may be appropriate in certain cases

4

Standard I: Professionalism

Standard I(A) Knowledge of the Law

Understand and comply with all laws, rules, and regulations (including Code and Standards) of any government, regulatory agency, or association governing professional activities

Comply with *more strict* law, rule, and regulation

Do not knowingly assist in violation, otherwise dissociate from activity

3

Standard I: Professionalism

Standard I(A) - Knowledge of the Law

Recommended Procedures

Keep informed, regularly review written compliance procedures, maintain files

Seek compliance/legal advice as needed

Encourage firms to adopt code of ethics

5

Standard I: Professionalism

Standard I(A) - Knowledge of the Law

Recommended Procedures

Distribute information internally on applicable laws and regulations

Have written procedures for reporting suspected violations

Members strongly encouraged to report violations by other members

6

Standard I: Professionalism

Standard I(B) - Independence and Objectivity

Use reasonable care, judgment to achieve and maintain independence in professional activities

Do not offer, solicit, or accept any compensation that could compromise independence or objectivity

7

Standard I: Professionalism

Standard I(B) - Independence and Objectivity

Guidance

Modest gifts okay

Distinguish between gifts from clients and gifts from entities trying to influence a member's behavior

May accept gift from clients—disclose to employer—get permission if for future performance

8

Standard I: Professionalism

Standard I(B) - Independence and Objectivity

Guidance

Members responsible for hiring outside managers should not accept travel, gifts, or entertainment that could impair their objectivity

Investment banking relationships—do not bow to pressure to issue favorable research

For issuer-paid research, flat fee structure is preferred; must disclose

© Kaplan, Inc.

9

Standard I: Professionalism

Standard I(B) - Independence and Objectivity

Guidance

Members working for credit rating firms should avoid influence by issuing firms

Users of credit ratings should be aware of this potential conflict

Best practice is for analysts to pay for their own commercial travel to firms being analyzed or to firm events

© Kaplan, Inc.

10

Standard I: Professionalism

Standard I(B) - Independence and Objectivity

Recommended Procedures

- Protect integrity of opinions—reports should reflect unbiased opinion
- Create a restricted list
- Restrict special cost arrangements
- Limit gifts; clear value limits by firm
- Be careful with IPO share allocations

© Kaplan, Inc.

11

Standard I: Professionalism

Standard I(C) - Misrepresentation

Do not make misrepresentations relating to investment analysis, recommendations, actions, or other professional activities

© Kaplan, Inc.

12

Standard I(C) - Misrepresentation
Guidance

- Standard covers oral, written, and electronic communications

- Do not misrepresent qualifications, services of self or firm, or performance record, characteristics of an investment

- Do not guarantee a certain return

- No plagiarism

© Kaplan, Inc.

13

Standard I(C) - Misrepresentation
Recommended Procedures

Firms can assist employees by providing written list of the firm's available services and a description of the firm's qualifications

Maintain records of materials used to prepare research reports, and quote source, except for "recognized financial and statistical reporting services"

© Kaplan, Inc.

14

Standard I(C) - Misrepresentation
Recommended Procedures

Models and analysis of others at the firm may be used without attribution

Should encourage firm to establish procedures for verifying marketing claims of third parties recommended to clients

© Kaplan, Inc.

15

Standard I(D) - Misconduct

Do not engage in any professional conduct involving dishonesty, fraud, deceit, or commit any act that reflects adversely on professional reputation, integrity, or competence

© Kaplan, Inc.

16

Standard I: Professionalism

Standard I(D) - Misconduct

Guidance

This Standard covers conduct that may not be illegal, but could adversely affect a member's ability to perform duties

© Kaplan, Inc.   17

Standard I: Professionalism

Standard I(D) - Misconduct

Recommended Procedures

- Adopt a code of ethics to which every employee must adhere
- Disseminate a list of potential violations and associated disciplinary sanctions
- Conduct background checks on potential employees—look for good character and eligibility to work in the investment industry

© Kaplan, Inc.   18

Ethical and Professional Standards

Standard II: Integrity of Capital Markets

KAPLAN UNIVERSITY | SCHOOL OF PROFESSIONAL AND CONTINUING EDUCATION | SCHWESER

Standard II: Integrity of Capital Markets

Standard II(A) Material Nonpublic Information

Members in possession of nonpublic information that could affect an investment's value must not act or cause someone else to act on the information

© Kaplan, Inc.   20

Standard II(A) Material Nonpublic Information
Guidance

"Material"—if disclosure of information would affect a security's price or if an investor would want to know before making an investment decision

If price effect is ambiguous, information may not be considered material

Extends to info such as upcoming rating change, influential analysis to be released

© Kaplan, Inc.

21

Standard II(A) Material Nonpublic Information
Guidance

Information is "nonpublic" until it has been made available to the marketplace

Information made available to analysts is considered nonpublic until it is made available to investors in general

"Act" includes related swaps and options, mutual funds with the security

© Kaplan, Inc.

22

Standard II(A) Material Nonpublic Information
Guidance

May use firm-provided information for certain specified purposes (e.g., due diligence for transactions with firm)

Mosaic Theory—no violation when an analyst combines nonmaterial, nonpublic information with public information to reach conclusion

© Kaplan, Inc.

23

Standard II(A) Material Nonpublic Information
Recommended Procedures

Information barrier or "firewall" is recommended to control interdepartmental communications

Information barrier includes use of restricted list

Review employee trades

© Kaplan, Inc.

24

Standard II: Integrity of Capital Markets

Standard II(A) Material Nonpublic Information

Recommended Procedures

Increase review/restrict proprietary trading while firm is in possession of material nonpublic information

© Kaplan, Inc.

25

Standard II: Integrity of Capital Markets

Standard II(B) Market Manipulation

Do not engage in practices that distort prices or artificially inflate trading volume with **intent to mislead** market participants

© Kaplan, Inc.

26

Standard II: Integrity of Capital Markets

Standard II(B) Market Manipulation

Guidance

Do not engage in transaction-based manipulation
- Giving false impression of activity/price movement
- Gaining dominant position in an asset to manipulate price of the asset or a related derivative

Do not distribute false, misleading information

© Kaplan, Inc.

27

Standard III:
Duties to Clients and
Prospective Clients

KAPLAN UNIVERSITY   SCHOOL OF PROFESSIONAL AND CONTINUING EDUCATION   SCHWESER

Standard III(A) – Loyalty, Prudence and Care

Duty of loyalty to clients—act with reasonable care and exercise prudent judgment

Act for benefit of clients and place their interests before employer's or own interests

Determine and comply with any applicable fiduciary duty

© Kaplan, Inc.

29

Standard III(A) – Loyalty, Prudence and Care

Guidance

Take investment actions in client's best interests

Exercise prudence, care, skill, and diligence that a person familiar with such matters would use

© Kaplan, Inc.

30

Standard III(A) – Loyalty, Prudence and Care

Guidance

Follow applicable fiduciary duty

"Client" may be investing public

Manage pools of client assets according to terms of governing documents

© Kaplan, Inc.

31

Standard III(A) – Loyalty, Prudence and Care

Guidance

Make investment decisions in context of total portfolio

Vote proxies responsibly and disclose proxy voting policies to clients

"Soft dollars" must benefit client

© Kaplan, Inc.

32

Standard III(A) – Loyalty, Prudence and Care

Recommended Procedures

- Follow rules and laws
- Establish client investment objectives
- Diversify
- Deal fairly with clients—investment actions
- Disclose all possible conflicts

© Kaplan, Inc.

33

Standard III(A) – Loyalty, Prudence and Care

Recommended Procedures

- Vote proxies in best interest of clients and ultimate beneficiaries
- Keep client information confidential
- Seek best trading execution for clients
- Place client interests first

© Kaplan, Inc.

34

Standard III(B) – Fair Dealing

Deal fairly and objectively with all clients when:

- Providing investment analysis
- Making investment recommendations
- Taking investment action
- Engaging in other professional activities

© Kaplan, Inc.

35

Standard III: Duties to Clients and Prospective Clients

Standard III(B) – Fair Dealing

Guidance

No discrimination against any clients when disseminating investment recommendations or taking investment action

Fair does not mean *equal*

© Kaplan, Inc.

36

Standard III: Duties to Clients and Prospective Clients

Standard III(B) – Fair Dealing

Guidance

Different levels of service are okay as long as disclosed and do not disadvantage any clients

All clients must have fair chance to act on every investment recommendation

If client is unaware of recommendation change, advise before accepting trade order

© Kaplan, Inc.

37

Standard III: Duties to Clients and Prospective Clients

Standard III(B) – Fair Dealing

Guidance

Treat all clients fairly—consider investment objectives and circumstances

Disclose written allocation procedures

Do not disadvantage any clients when distributing "hot" issues

© Kaplan, Inc.

38

Standard III: Duties to Clients and Prospective Clients

Standard III(B) – Fair Dealing

Recommended Procedures

Limit number of people aware of upcoming changes

Shorten time frame—decision to dissemination

Have pre-dissemination guidelines

Simultaneous dissemination

© Kaplan, Inc.

39

Standard III: Duties to Clients and Prospective Clients

Standard III(B) – Fair Dealing

Recommended Procedures

Maintain list of clients and their holdings

Disclose trade allocation procedures

Review accounts regularly to ensure fair client treatment

© Kaplan, Inc.

40

Standard III: Duties to Clients and Prospective Clients

Standard III(B) – Fair Dealing

Recommended Procedures

If firm offers different levels of service, disclose this fact to all clients

Deviations from strict pro rata allocation of IPO is sometimes okay (e.g., minimum block sizes)

© Kaplan, Inc.

41

Standard III: Duties to Clients and Prospective Clients

Standard III(C) – Suitability

When in advisory relationship with a client:

- Make reasonable inquiry as to client's investment experience, risk/return objectives, financial constraints prior to making any recommendation, or taking investment action
- Update information regularly

© Kaplan, Inc.

42

Standard III: Duties to Clients and Prospective Clients

Standard III(C) – Suitability

When in advisory relationship with client:

- Ensure investment is suitable to client's situation and consistent with written objectives before recommending an investment or taking investment action
- Look at suitability in a portfolio context

© Kaplan, Inc.

43

Standard III: Duties to Clients and Prospective Clients

Standard III(C) – Suitability

When responsible for managing a portfolio to a specific mandate, strategy, or style, only make recommendations or take investment actions that are consistent with the stated objectives and constraints of the portfolio

© Kaplan, Inc.

44

Standard III: Duties to Clients and Prospective Clients

Standard III(C) – Suitability

Guidance

- When in advisory relationship, gather client information at the outset and prepare IPS
- Update IPS at least annually
- Consider whether leverage (derivatives) is suitable for client
- If managing a fund to an index or other mandate, invest according to mandate

© Kaplan, Inc.

45

Standard III: Duties to Clients and Prospective Clients

Standard III(C) – Suitability

Guidance

If a client requests an unsuitable trade, discuss suitability with the client before executing

- If not material to portfolio, follow firm's policies for client approval
- If material, discuss whether IPS needs update
- If client declines to update IPS, follow firm's policies or reconsider advisory relationship

© Kaplan, Inc.

46

Standard III: Duties to Clients and Prospective Clients

Standard III(C) – Suitability

Recommended Procedures

When formulating IPS for client, know the client's:

- Return objectives
- Risk tolerance

© Kaplan, Inc.

47

Standard III(C) – Suitability

Recommended Procedures

Determine the client's constraints:

- Liquidity needs
- Expected cash flows, investable funds
- Time horizon, tax considerations
- Regulatory/legal constraints
- Unique circumstances/needs

© Kaplan, Inc.

48

Standard III(D) – Performance Presentation

When communicating investment performance information, make reasonable efforts to ensure that it is fair, accurate, and complete

Can make brief presentation, note limited nature, and make detailed information available on request

© Kaplan, Inc.

49

Standard III(D) – Performance Presentation

Guidance

- Do not misstate performance or mislead clients about investment performance
- Do not misrepresent past performance
- Provide fair and complete performance information
- Do not state or imply ability to achieve returns similar to those achieved in the past

© Kaplan, Inc.

50

Standard III(D) – Performance Presentation

Recommended Procedures

- Consider audience sophistication when presenting performance
- Use performance of the weighted composite of similar portfolios
- Include terminated accounts as part of historical performance
- Make all disclosures and maintain records

© Kaplan, Inc.

51

Standard III: Duties to Clients and Prospective Clients

Standard III(E) – Confidentiality

Keep current and prospective client information confidential, unless:

- Illegal activities are suspected
- Disclosure is required by law
- Client or prospect allows disclosure of the information

© Kaplan, Inc.

52

Standard III: Duties to Clients and Prospective Clients

Standard III(E) – Confidentiality

Guidance

In some cases it may be required by law to report activities to relevant authorities

This Standard extends to former clients

Exception: May provide confidential information to CFA Institute for an investigation under Professional Conduct Program

© Kaplan, Inc.

53

Standard III: Duties to Clients and Prospective Clients

Standard III(E) – Confidentiality

Recommended Procedures

Avoid discussing any information received from a client except to colleagues working on the same project

Follow firm's electronic data storage procedures; recommend adoption of procedures if none exist

© Kaplan, Inc.

54

Ethical and Professional Standards

Standard IV:
Duties to Employers

KAPLAN UNIVERSITY | SCHOOL OF PROFESSIONAL AND CONTINUING EDUCATION | **SCHWESER**

Standard IV: Duties to Employers

Standard IV(A) – Loyalty

On matters related to employment, act for benefit of employer and do not deprive employer of the advantage of skills/abilities, divulge confidential information, or otherwise cause harm to employer

© Kaplan, Inc.

56

Standard IV: Duties to Employers

Standard IV(A) – Loyalty
Guidance

Place client interests first but consider effects on firm integrity and sustainability

Members encouraged to give employer a copy of the Code and Standards

No incentive or compensation structure that encourages unethical behavior

© Kaplan, Inc.

57

Standard IV: Duties to Employers

Standard IV(A) – Loyalty
Guidance

Independent Practice:

- If planning to engage in independent practice, notify employer of services provided, expected duration, and compensation

- Do not proceed without consent from employer

© Kaplan, Inc.

58

Standard IV: Duties to Employers

Standard IV(A) – Loyalty
Guidance

Leaving an Employer:

- Act in best interest of employer until resignation is effective
- Employer records on any medium (e.g., cell phone, PDA, home computer) are property of the firm
- Simple knowledge of names of former clients is okay; but don't solicit prior to leaving
- No prohibition on use of experience or knowledge gained at former employer

© Kaplan, Inc.

59

Standard IV: Duties to Employers

Standard IV(A) – Loyalty

Guidance

Whistleblowing:

- Permitted only if it protects client or integrity of capital markets
- Not permitted for personal gain

© Kaplan, Inc.

60

Standard IV: Duties to Employers

Standard IV(A) – Loyalty

Recommended Practices

Encourage firms to adopt policies regarding:

- Outside practice, non-compete agreements
- Leaving employer (resignation, termination)
- Incident reporting
- Employee classification (full-time, part-time, contractor)

© Kaplan, Inc.

61

Standard IV: Duties to Employers

Standard IV(B) – Additional Compensation

Do not accept gifts, benefits, compensation, or consideration that competes with, or creates a conflict of interest with, employer's interest unless written consent is obtained from all parties involved

© Kaplan, Inc.

62

Standard IV: Duties to Employers

Standard IV(B) – Additional Compensation

Guidance

Compensation and benefits covers direct compensation by the client and other benefits received from third parties

For written consent from "all parties involved," email is acceptable

© Kaplan, Inc.

63

Standard IV: Duties to Employers

Standard IV(B) – Additional Compensation

Recommended Procedures

- Written report to employer with details of proposed compensation in addition to normal compensation and benefits
  - Details of incentives verified by offering party
  - Include nature of compensation, amount, and duration of agreement

64

Standard IV: Duties to Employers

Standard IV(C) – Responsibilities of Supervisors

Make reasonable efforts to ensure that anyone subject to your supervision or authority complies with applicable laws, rules, regulations, and Code and Standards

65

Standard IV: Duties to Employers

Standard IV(C) – Responsibilities of Supervisors

Guidance

Supervisors must take steps to prevent employees from violating laws, rules, regulations, or the Code and Standards

Supervisors must make reasonable efforts to detect violations

66

Standard IV: Duties to Employers

Standard IV(C) – Responsibilities of Supervisors

Recommended Procedures

Adequate compliance procedures should:
- Be clear and understandable
- Designate a compliance officer
- Have checks/balances; permitted conduct
- Have procedures for reporting violations

67

Standard IV(C) – Responsibilities of Supervisors

Recommended Procedures

Supervisor and compliance officer should:

- Distribute procedures; update periodically
- Continually educate staff
- Review employee actions
- Promptly initiate procedures once a violation has occurred

© Kaplan, Inc.

68

Standard IV(C) – Responsibilities of Supervisors

Recommended Procedures

Once a violation has occurred, a supervisor should:

- Respond promptly
- Conduct a thorough investigation
- Place appropriate limitations on the wrongdoer until investigation is complete

© Kaplan, Inc.

69

Ethical and Professional Standards

Standard V: Investment Analysis, Recommendations, and Actions

KAPLAN UNIVERSITY SCHOOL OF PROFESSIONAL AND CONTINUING EDUCATION | SCHWESER

Standard V: Investment Analysis, Recommendations, and Actions

Standard V(A) – Diligence and Reasonable Basis

Exercise diligence, independence, thoroughness in analyzing investments, making investment recommendations, and taking investment action

Have a reasonable and adequate basis, supported by research, for analysis, recommendation, or action

© Kaplan, Inc.

71

Standard V: Investment Analysis, Recommendations, and Actions

Standard V(A) – Diligence and Reasonable Basis
Guidance

Make reasonable efforts to cover all relevant issues when arriving at an investment recommendation

Level of diligence will depend on product or service offered

© Kaplan, Inc.

72

Standard V: Investment Analysis, Recommendations, and Actions

Standard V(A) – Diligence and Reasonable Basis
Guidance

Using secondary or third-party research:

- Determine soundness of the research—review assumptions, rigor, timeliness, and independence
- Encourage firm to adopt policy of periodic review of quality of third-party research: assumptions, timeliness, rigor, objectivity, and independence

© Kaplan, Inc.

73

Standard V: Investment Analysis, Recommendations, and Actions

Standard V(A) – Diligence and Reasonable Basis
Recommended Procedures

Establish policy that research and recommendations should have reasonable and adequate basis

Review/approve research reports and recommendations prior to external circulation

© Kaplan, Inc.

74

Standard V: Investment Analysis, Recommendations, and Actions

Standard V(A) – Diligence and Reasonable Basis
Recommended Procedures

Establish due diligence procedures for judging if recommendation has met reasonable and adequate basis criteria

Develop measurable criteria for assessing quality of research

© Kaplan, Inc.

75

Standard V: Investment Analysis, Recommendations, and Actions

Standard V(A) – Diligence and Reasonable Basis
Recommended Procedures

Consider scenarios outside recent experience to assess downside risk of quantitative models

Make sure firm has procedures to evaluate external advisers they use or promote, including how often to review

© Kaplan, Inc.

76

Standard V: Investment Analysis, Recommendations, and Actions

Standard V(A) – Diligence and Reasonable Basis
Recommended Procedures

- Written procedures of acceptable scenario testing, range of scenarios, cash flow sensitivity to assumptions and inputs
- Procedure for evaluating outside information providers including how often
  - No need to dissociate from group research that the member disagrees with

© Kaplan, Inc.

77

Standard V: Investment Analysis, Recommendations, and Actions

Standard V(B) – Communication with Clients and Prospective Clients

Disclose basic format/general principles of investment processes used to analyze investments, select securities, and construct portfolios

Promptly disclose any changes that may affect those processes materially

© Kaplan, Inc.

78

Standard V: Investment Analysis, Recommendations, and Actions

Standard V(B) – Communication with Clients and Prospective Clients

Disclose risks and limitations (e.g., liquidity, capacity) associated with investment process

- Use reasonable judgment in identifying which factors are important to investment analyses, recommendations, or actions
  - Include those factors in communications with clients/prospective clients

© Kaplan, Inc.

79

Standard V: Investment Analysis, Recommendations, and Actions

Standard V(B) – Communication with Clients and Prospective Clients

Distinguish between fact and opinion in presentation of investment analysis and investment recommendations

Clearly communicate potential gains and losses on an investment

© Kaplan, Inc.

80

Standard V: Investment Analysis, Recommendations, and Actions

Standard V(B) – Communication with Clients and Prospective Clients

Guidance

Include basic characteristics of the security

Inform clients of any change in investment processes

Suitability of investment—portfolio context

All communication covered, not just reports

© Kaplan, Inc.

81

Standard V: Investment Analysis, Recommendations, and Actions

Standard V(B) – Communication with Clients and Prospective Clients

Recommended Procedures

The inclusion or exclusion of information depends on a case-by-case review

Maintain records

82

© Kaplan, Inc.

Standard V: Investment Analysis, Recommendations, and Actions

Standard V(C) – Record Retention

Develop and maintain appropriate records to support investment analyses, recommendations, actions, and other investment-related communications with clients and prospective clients

83

© Kaplan, Inc.

Standard V: Investment Analysis, Recommendations, and Actions

Standard V(C) – Record Retention

Guidance

- Maintain records to support research, and the rationale for conclusions and actions
- Records are firm's property and cannot be taken when member leaves without firm's consent
- If no regulatory requirement or firm policy, CFA Institute recommends retention period of 7 years

84

© Kaplan, Inc.

Standard V: Investment Analysis, Recommendations, and Actions

Standard V(C) – Record Retention

Recommended Procedures

Responsibility to maintain records generally falls with the firm

However, individuals must retain documents that support investment-related communications

85

© Kaplan, Inc.

Ethical and Professional Standards

Standard VI:
Conflicts of Interest

Standard V: Investment Analysis, Recommendations, and Actions

Standard V(C) – Record Retention

Recommended Procedures

When member changes firm, must recreate records from public sources and new firm's information (can't rely on memory or materials from old firm)

86

Standard VI: Conflicts of Interest

Standard VI(A) – Disclosure of Conflicts

Guidance

Disclose to clients:

- All matters that could impair objectivity—allow clients to judge motives, biases
  - For example, between member or firm and issuer, investment banking relations, broker/dealer market-making activities, significant stock ownership, board service

89

Standard VI: Conflicts of Interest

Standard VI(A) – Disclosure of Conflicts

Make full, fair disclosure of all matters that could reasonably be expected to impair independence/objectivity, or interfere with duties to clients, prospects, or employer

Ensure disclosures are prominent, delivered in plain language

88

Standard VI(A) – Disclosure of Conflicts

Guidance

Disclose to employers:

- Conflicts of interest—ownership of stock analyzed/recommended, board participation, financial and other pressures that may influence decisions
- Also covers conflicts that could be damaging to employer's business

© Kaplan, Inc.

90

Standard VI(A) – Disclosure of Conflicts

Recommended Procedures

Disclose compensation arrangements with employer that conflict with clients' interests

If firm does not permit disclosure, consider dissociating from the activity

Firms are encouraged to include compensation information in promotional materials

© Kaplan, Inc.

91

Standard VI(B) – Priority of Transactions

Investment transactions for clients and employers must have priority over transactions in which a member or candidate is the beneficial owner

Do not use knowledge of pending trades for personal gain

© Kaplan, Inc.

92

Standard VI(B) – Priority of Transactions

Guidance

- "Beneficial owner"—has direct/indirect personal interest in the securities
- Client, employer transactions take priority over personal transactions (including beneficial ownership)
- Family member accounts that are client accounts must be treated as other client accounts

© Kaplan, Inc.

93

Standard VI: Conflicts of Interest

Standard VI(B) – Priority of Transactions

Recommended Procedures

Firm's compliance procedures should:

- Limit participation in equity IPOs
- Restrict purchase of securities through private placements

Standard VI: Conflicts of Interest

Standard VI(B) – Priority of Transactions

Recommended Procedures

Establish blackout/restricted periods

Establish reporting procedures and prior clearance requirements

Disclose policies on personal investing to clients, upon request

Standard VI: Conflicts of Interest

Standard VI(C) – Referral Fees

Disclose to employer, clients, and prospective clients, as appropriate, any compensation, consideration, benefit received from, or paid to, others for the recommendation of products or services

Standard VI: Conflicts of Interest

Standard VI(C) – Referral Fees

Guidance

Disclosure allows clients and employers to evaluate full cost of service and any potential biases

Disclosure is to be made prior to entering into any formal agreement for services

Disclose the nature of the consideration

Ethical and Professional Standards

Standard VII:
Responsibilities as a CFA Institute Member or CFA Candidate

KAPLAN UNIVERSITY | SCHOOL OF PROFESSIONAL AND CONTINUING EDUCATION | SCHWESER

Standard VI: Conflicts of Interest

Standard VI(C) – Referral Fees

Guidance

Encourage firm to have clear policy regarding referral compensation

Firms that do not prohibit should have clear approval process

Members should update referral compensation disclosure to employer at least quarterly

© Kaplan, Inc.

98

Standard VII: Responsibilities as a CFA Institute Member or Candidate

Standard VII(A) – Conduct as Participants in CFA Institute Programs

Guidance

Conduct includes:

- Cheating on the exam
- Disregarding rules and policies or security measures related to exam administration
- Giving confidential information to candidates or public

© Kaplan, Inc.

101

Standard VII: Responsibilities as a CFA Institute Member or Candidate

Standard VII(A) – Conduct as Participants in CFA Institute Programs

Do not engage in any conduct that compromises the reputation or integrity of CFA Institute or CFA designation, or the integrity, validity, or security of CFA Institute programs

© Kaplan, Inc.

100

Standard VII(A) – Conduct as Participants in CFA Institute Programs

Guidance

Don't disclose:

- Formulas tested or not tested on exam
- Specific question information
- Topic emphasis on the exam or topics tested

© Kaplan, Inc.

103

Standard VII(B) – Reference to CFA Institute, the CFA Designation, and the CFA Program

Guidance

CFA Institute membership:

- Complete PCS annually
- Pay membership dues annually
- Failure to comply with above results in an inactive member status

© Kaplan, Inc.

105

Standard VII(A) – Conduct as Participants in CFA Institute Programs

Guidance

Conduct includes (continued):

- Improper use of CFA designation to further personal and professional objectives
- Misrepresenting the CFA Institute Professional Development Program or the Professional Conduct Statement

© Kaplan, Inc.

102

Standard VII(B) – Reference to CFA Institute, the CFA Designation, and the CFA Program

When referring to CFA Institute, membership, designation, or candidacy, do not misrepresent or exaggerate the meaning or implications of membership in CFA Institute, holding the CFA designation, or candidacy in the CFA program

© Kaplan, Inc.

104

Standard VII(B) – Reference to CFA Institute, the CFA Designation, and the CFA Program

Guidance

Use the marks "Chartered Financial Analyst" or "CFA" in a manner that does not misrepresent or exaggerate the meaning or implications of holding the CFA designation

© Kaplan, Inc.

106

Standard VII(B) – Reference to CFA Institute, the CFA Designation, and the CFA Program

Guidance

Reference to the CFA program:

- Candidates may reference participation in CFA program, but do not imply achievement of any type of partial designation
  - Okay to say "passed all levels on first attempt," but do not imply superior ability

© Kaplan, Inc.

107

Standard VII(B) – Reference to CFA Institute, the CFA Designation, and the CFA Program

Guidance

Improper use of the CFA marks:

- The "Chartered Financial Analyst" and "CFA" marks must always be used either after a charterholder's name or as adjectives, not nouns
- Do not use the CFA designation in pseudonyms or online names that hide identity

© Kaplan, Inc.

108

Standard VII(B) – Reference to CFA Institute, the CFA Designation, and the CFA Program

Recommended Procedures

Make sure that your employer is aware of the proper references to the CFA designation and CFA candidacy

© Kaplan, Inc.

109

Ethical and Professional Standards

Introduction to the Global Investment Performance Standards (GIPS®)

KAPLAN UNIVERSITY | SCHOOL OF PROFESSIONAL AND CONTINUING EDUCATION | SCHWESER

Why GIPS Were Created

GIPS make performance measurement among firms comparable, with standardized calculation and reporting practices

GIPS aim to avoid misrepresentation of performance of investment firms and to give clients relevant information to evaluate past performance

© Kaplan, Inc.

2

Parties Affected by GIPS

Firms—the GIPS apply to investment management firms

Prospective and current clients—intended to serve prospective and current clients of investment management firms

© Kaplan, Inc.

3

Composites: Construction and Purpose

Composite—grouping of individual discretionary portfolios with same investment strategy, objective, or mandate

A composite must include all portfolios (current and past) that the firm has managed in accordance with this particular strategy

Groupings must be pre-identified

© Kaplan, Inc.

4

Purpose of Verification

Voluntarily, a firm may hire an independent third party to verify its claim of GIPS compliance

Primary purpose of verification is to provide assurance that compliance with GIPS is on a firm-wide basis

© Kaplan, Inc.   5

Requirements for Verification

If a firm chooses verification, it must be performed by a third party on a firm-wide basis

Verifier must attest that firm has complied with GIPS requirements for composite construction, and firm's processes/procedures are established to present performance in accordance with proper calculation methods, data, and format

© Kaplan, Inc.   6

Ethics and Professional Standards

Ethical and Professional Standards

The GIPS Standards

KAPLAN UNIVERSITY SCHOOL OF PROFESSIONAL AND CONTINUING EDUCATION | SCHWESER

LOS 4.a Describe

The GIPS Standards

GIPS Objectives

- Obtain global acceptance of calculation and presentation standards—fair, comparable format with full disclosure
- Ensure consistent, accurate performance data—reporting, marketing, presentations
- Promote fair competition
- Promote global industry "self-regulation"

© Kaplan, Inc.

2

LOS 4.a Describe

The GIPS Standards

GIPS Key Characteristics

- To claim compliance, define firm—"distinct" business entity
- GIPS—ethical standards for performance presentation—ensure fair representation
- Include all actual fee-paying, discretionary portfolios in composites for 5-year minimum, or since inception (add performance results each year—10 years)

© Kaplan, Inc.

3

LOS 4.a Describe

The GIPS Standards

GIPS Key Characteristics (continued)

- Certain calculation/presentation standards are required, along with disclosures
- Input data must be accurate
- GIPS—required and recommended provisions (encouraged)
- No partial compliance allowed
- If GIPS conflicts with local law, follow local law, but disclose conflict

© Kaplan, Inc.

4

The GIPS Standards

GIPS Claim of Compliance

Once GIPS requirements are met:

"[Firm name] has prepared and presented this report in compliance with the Global Investment Performance Standards (GIPS)"

No statements referring to calculation methodologies used in a composite presentation being "in accordance with GIPS"

© Kaplan, Inc.

5

The GIPS Standards

GIPS Firm's Fundamental Responsibilities

- Provide compliant presentation to all prospects
- Provide composite list/description to all prospects who make a request
- On client request, provide compliant presentation and composite description
- Joint marketing, separate non-compliant firm

© Kaplan, Inc.

6

The GIPS Standards

Firm Definition and Historical Record

To claim compliance, firm defined as the "distinct **business entity**" held out to clients

Include all **actual fee-paying, discretionary portfolios** in composites for a minimum of **five years** or since <u>firm or composite inception</u>

Must add one year of compliant performance history each year until a 10-year record is presented

© Kaplan, Inc.

7

The GIPS Standards

Countries With Existing Standards

Firms that previously represented performance in compliance with a specific Country Version of GIPS (CVG) may claim GIPS compliance prior to January 1, 2006

In cases where country-specific regulations are different from GIPS, follow the country-specific regulations, but disclose the nature of the conflict with GIPS

© Kaplan, Inc.

8

The GIPS Standards

LOS 4.d Describe

9 Major Sections of GIPS

0. *Fundamentals of compliance*—issues for firms to consider when claiming GIPS compliance, including definition of firm

1. *Input data*—must be consistent, for full, fair, comparable performance presentations

2. *Calculation methodology*—certain methodologies are required; be uniform in methods

9

The GIPS Standards

LOS 4.d Describe

9 Major Sections of GIPS (continued)

3. *Composite construction*—create meaningful, asset-weighted composites

4. *Disclosures*—certain info must be disclosed about presentation/policies

5. *Presentation and reporting*—present investment performance according to GIPS requirements

10

The GIPS Standards

LOS 4.d Describe

9 Major Sections of GIPS (continued)

6. *Real estate*—provisions also apply to real estate investments, regardless of level of control the firm has over management of the investment

7. *Private equity*—value according to GIPS Private Equity Valuation Principles, unless open-end or evergreen fund (then follow regular GIPS)

11

The GIPS Standards

LOS 4.d Describe

9 Major Sections of GIPS (continued)

8. *Wrap Fee/Separately Managed Account (SMA) Portfolios*—a supplement to Sections 0–5 with specific reference to those provisions that don't apply to Wrap Fee/SMA portfolios and some provisions here that supersede those in Sections 0–5

12

Notes

Notes

Notes

Notes

Notes

Notes